The Path To Million Dollar Production

Patti Branco

Insight Publishing
Sevierville, Tennessee

The Path To

Million Dollar Production

Printed in the United States of America

1 0 9 8 7 6 5 4 3 2

ISBN-13. 978-1-60013

ISBN-10: 1-60013-150-6

Published by Insight Publishing
P.O. Box 4189
Sevierville, TN 37864

Dedication

For
Michael Branco, my soul mate who encourages me to embrace life to the fullest,

for
Kathi White, my best fan and favorite pal

for
Melissa Smith, life's greatest gift, my 'number one'

Thank you all for your support and love!

And for all the many people throughout the past twenty plus years who have been directly and indirectly responsible for the amazing success I have enjoyed, thank you for believing in me. You know who you are.

Table of Contents

". . . There is a place for everyone, man and woman, old and young, hale and halt; service in a thousand forms is open. There is no room now for the dilettante, the weakling, for the shirker, or the sluggard. . . . From the highest to the humblest tasks, all are of equal honor; all have their part to play."

—Winston Churchill (1874–1965)

Introduction

There are many paths to becoming a million dollar producer. You may be a rookie, eagerly grasping all the ideas you can handle. Perhaps you are a rep in a bank or credit union. You may be a tenured and successful broker who needs a "tune up." You may be a seasoned wirehouse broker who is merely stuck or at a plateau. You're doing many of the things we cover, but missing one or two, and that could make all the difference! Perhaps you are a superstar promoted to new manger and looking for leadership pointers and business building tactics to share with your team. Wherever you are on your path, there is something for you in this book. This is "The way" to Million Dollar production.

The only thing you need to bring to the table is the same enthusiasm you had the day you entered this business. Do you remember the thrill of passing those exams, and seeing business cards that named you a "financial advisor"? How about that guy in the office who drove a Lamborghini to work, and the gal building a home on oceanfront property? *"I can do this," you thought.*

You need to unlearn regretful habits and transport your emotions to that first opportunity. *You* can *do this!*

Why is Patti Branco qualified to write this book?

She knows this business. This book is based on twenty-five years of solid success and broad experience in a variety of channels in the financial services industry. Patti has been in your seat, in your manager's seat, and in his manager's seat. She has helped hundreds of firms build a successful investment program model and thousands of individuals prosper in this business.

Within the pages of this book lies the gift of her knowledge enjoyed by thousands of individuals—from wirehouse brokerages to insurance firms to banks and credit unions—who are now successful.

Many books are written for you by talented consultants who devise clever and complicated programs with unique spin, but few can claim the depth of experience Patti Branco enjoys; a twenty-five-year stellar track record in both retail selling, senior management, and consulting. It's simple—it's not easy, it's sometimes challenging, but it is simple.

You will see a variety of terms to describe the financial professional who sells insurance and investments. Rep, advisor, registered rep, stockbroker, financial planner, agent—they all mean the same thing for the purposes of this book. Many of the ideas and best practices translate to other professions, but this book is for the registered representative, one of the most rewarding professions in the world.

So roll up your sleeves and get ready to work, the rest is all about you!

The Path To
Million Dollar Production

The Path to Million Dollar Production

Warning: The way to unparalleled success for Investment Reps, Managers, Future Managers, and Team Leaders in all channels of the financial services industry requires your willingness to work as never before!

Investment Sales—More Art than Science

This book is about the investment business, which as complicated as it may seem, with all the many venues where investments are now sold, and all the different designations available to promote registered reps. It is really simple. It's not easy—challenging, sure; but it is simple.

It is challenging because there are so many steps and competencies needed to accomplish that goal to a level of brilliance that generates a million dollars in gross commission per year. Add in the fact that today's seventy-six million Baby Boomers are a far more savvy, self-educated, and media exposed generation when it comes to the world of the financial services, and they expect the very best from their preferred advisor.

It is simple because your number one job responsibility is to see people who need or want assistance with their investments, recommend a solution when appropriate, and ask for the business that results in a sale. It is wise to keep this uppermost in your mind. That's the simple part—one that is so often forgotten or avoided. This is called *selling!*

Selling is usually the most personally difficult in light of all other responsibilities a rep has. Filing, research, seminar preparation, networking, paperwork, marketing, meetings, and other "busy" activities are painless. Selling means possible rejection; but not selling (for whatever reasons) causes you to be indecisive and means failure.

You can speak about investments to a potential client until you are blue in the face, but at some point a sale takes place or the prospect leaves thinking he or she had a wonderful, informational (and uneventful) meeting!

Many moons ago I learned to close when I met a lovely older lady at an airport. We were sitting next to each other and she was holding a very dog-eared prospectus that she was mulling over. We chatted a bit and she began to tell me everything about the investment she had in her hand—I mean *everything!* Being an experienced registered rep myself I asked if she had invested in it. She answered, "No, my fellow at the bank *didn't put me in it."*

He didn't close. He spent an hour with her, she took notes, and she thought this was a terrific fund. Then he said goodbye and off she went. I immediately thought of all the wonderful presentations I had done, and how I would wait for the client to tell me they just had to have this product or service! After this chance meeting with this smart old gal, I changed my approach and began to "put people in it" when it was appropriate and suitable. My business doubled. This is a true confession!

So first and foremost a successful rep must sell, close sales, open accounts. . . and the reps who can't (or won't) wash out to the ratio of about 30 percent. The good news is there is hope for everyone if they are actively engaged in the business, willing to change, and open to new ideas.

This book is about selling, closing sales, launching new relationships, creating dynamic teams, and building a million dollar practice with integrity and life balance. It will cover many issues that are ancillary to sales and critical for one's success, such as fitting within your firm's culture, getting along with your manager, being well acquainted with your products and services, managing yourself and your time effectively, having the ability to pay attention to detail, and the importance of operational reliability. There is also a section on leadership for branch managers and team leaders.

There is wisdom and direction for all areas of the financial services industry, all geared to increase production in a compliant and supportive environment, and often overlooked in most training manuals.

Finding Qualified Clients

If the same old thing isn't bringing in results, maybe it's time to vary your strategy. Top producing advisors use a variety of ways to get themselves in front of some new prospects!

The financial services industry is a fierce place to be. Natural selection leaves behind the bones of many once-mighty business and selling models. A chameleon-like ability to adapt to changing environments is essential for the broker to survive. Whether he is a wirehouse advisor, a bank or credit union rep, an insurance specialist or an independent broker—the rules have definitely changed.

Unless you inherited "Uncle Harry's bulging book of clients," this presents your first nerve-racking challenge as a new advisor or a tenured advisor trying to get to the next illusive level of business.

The good news is that there are plenty of potential clients who would welcome your advice. The bad news is that you have to find them. I feel cold-calling is almost impossible these days due to privacy regulations and "do-not-call-lists," aside from the fact that it is one of the biggest de-motivating activities invented. If it is a requirement by your manager, the only way around it is to replace cold-calling with something else that works.

If the market uncertainty and cold-calling has you paralyzed with procrastination, shake off your indecision by doing something different. While others stare at their computer screens and whine about how tough business is, you can get busy! Try a few of these proven and extraordinary ways to market yourself. The amazing thing is that just the very act of trying and being active seems to generate results regardless of the activity. Busy-ness fuels business!

The following few pages comprise over twenty ways that have proven successful for many top producers to land new accounts, and will work for you as well. A little negotiating and a positive result should help you convince your branch manager that there are ways to find prospects other than calling strangers during dinner time.

Finding Qualified Clients—20 Proven Ways!

Volunteering

Giving back has a twofold benefit. It allows you to help an organization that tugs at your heartstrings, and at the same time you meet people who are potential clients. Most people like to do business with someone they know, and volunteering opens a world of opportunities as well as a chance to meet gregarious people. A quick caveat here: never become active for the sole reason of meeting prospective clients; your insincerity will show and your whole purpose will be defeated. This is a good avenue only if you have the right reason for doing so.

Offer Complimentary Financial Plans

Product sales and a transactional approach served up remarkable success for the masses in the mid-eighties; a bull market in the nineties made wealthy brokers and advisors feel invincible. Today the emphasis is on deeper relationships, full service, client satisfaction, and everything in between supported by the required adage, “Know your customer.” *Client retention* is the strategic ‘buzzword’. The ability to recognize and adapt to change is a significant required proficiency. Becoming properly licensed to offer plans (CFP, 65 or 66) and offering them at no cost is a great tool to draw in new business, a worthy goal, and a way to earn the entire financial relationship.

Cold Walking

Getting out of the office one day a week, visiting local businesses or professional offices with cards and brochures for the purpose of introducing yourself can reap rewards. If you have the outgoing personality to do this with panache, enthusiasm, and an upbeat attitude, you will find yourself with interested prospects and maybe even some company retirement accounts. Many new busy startups haven’t thought about adding a 401k to the benefit plan or may not have been ready to do so until they met you! If you find it hard to get past the “gatekeeper,” try bringing him or her a sandwich at lunch time or a plant or even a candy bar. Above all, be respectful—it works wonders!

Become a Teacher

Give back to your community and get a captive audience at the same time. Apply to your local college or adult school and offer to teach a class on investing and estate planning. They are always looking for new talent. You don’t have to be a professor and you will find that people who attend a class on how to invest usually have the funds to do so! Keep the title of the class you teach pithy and interesting. Know your material well. This can be a one-time shot or an ongoing arrangement and often provides free advertising.

Affinity Markets

Do you have a favorite hobby such as golf, fishing, sailing, or skydiving? Do you have expertise in a former industry where you once worked? Those should be your first targets! Look into every aspect of people's interests and affiliate yourself with relevant associations. Read their magazines, become the niche expert and don't be afraid to reach out. People like to do business with someone they know.

Write Articles

Get some press and credibility by submitting articles to your local paper. Don't think you are the finest writer? Write a draft and have it edited by a local copyeditor. It is a well-kept secret that local newspapers are usually in need of articles, particularly in difficult times, and will welcome a submission from a local investment expert. If you would rather not tackle writing them yourself, most brokerage firms have an arrangement through their marketing department with a ghost writing service where the articles are already NASD filed and many are pretty good! You may submit under your name and get credit for them, however. If you Google "ghost written articles," several pages of eager authors pop up!

Become a Speaker

Present yourself to local associations and business organizations in town and offer to speak at a meeting. You can also offer to be a "speaker on call" for speakers who cancel at the last minute. When this happens, you'll be a hero.

Speak on a topic that you feel you know best—estate planning, saving for college, retirement planning, or anything pertinent to the investment industry. Prepare a short presentation in advance, pepper it with humor and a story or two, be ready to deliver it on a moments notice, and make sure it is not an infomercial. Just the very act of standing there and delivering a terrific presentation will make you the expert, no need to tell them you are. Not the best speaker? Join your local Toastmasters where you can learn to be a pro and meet new prospects too! www.ToastMastersInternational.org

Church Talks

Heed the calling to serve local parishioners. Behind the scenes, most churches are run like a business. There are bills to pay, lights to keep lit, and support staff needed to run the church. Offer to do a fundraiser, a content-rich presentation on effective money management for the congregation. Charge ten bucks. The church gets the money; the crowd gets your expertise and your business card. You get the clients.

Clip for Business

Scan newspapers with scissors in hand. Clip out articles or press releases of people you would like to do business with and send it to them with your card and a simple note, "Thought you might like a copy of this. Congratulations."

Corporate Directories

Securing a corporate directory for a firm that is experiencing layoffs is the best list one could ever want. Ask clients and friends for help in locating a corporate directory for a target firm and then ask their HR department for permission to assist in the informational/separation meetings they usually hold. Often the human resource department will welcome a helping hand in informing terminated employees of their options, so keep it above board, generic, and professional.

Launch an E-zine

A weekly e-mail update can generate a lot of inquiries. Start your own using the many informative pieces available from your firm or vendors. Keep it real short and sweet—e-mail newsletters get read if they are a quick read and about hot topics. Bullets points are even better. The point is to keep your name in from of them. A popular turnkey newsletter firm is

Emerald Publications, www.emeraldseminars.com. An excellent affordable distribution service that is user friendly (at the time of this writing) is Constant Contact, www.constantcontact.com.

Press Releases

If you receive a promotion or some other noteworthy award, send press releases to your local papers and to industry magazines; get the recognition you deserve as well as free PR. What a lot of people don't realize is that papers that have to print a publication every day or even weekly appreciate space fillers.

PowerPoint Marketing

Learn how to use Microsoft PowerPoint and create a dynamic brochure for your services that can be e-mailed, or saved on a disc and postage mailed. Just three or four informational slides create a unique, dramatic visual and the opportunity to learn a new skill.

Radio Talk Shows

Much like newspapers, radio shows look for guests with an interesting slant. What's yours? Find a unique selling proposition—your "USP"—call the radio stations and ask to speak to the program coordinator. Pay attention, the people you speak with listening to your voice, your tone, and your tempo!

Scripting

Here are five must-have scripts (fine-tune yours when things are slow!). Make sure your ten-second introduction and your thirty-second personal commercial are not about how wonderful you are and what fabulous schools you attended; but rather, what specific benefits you afford your clients. (More on scripting later.)

1. Ten-second introduction
2. Thirty-second personal commercial

3. Prospecting script
4. Product presentation script
5. Profiling script

Sponsor a Company or Church Picnic

Find a lucrative small business and offer to sponsor a company picnic. You might be able to get help from your favorite vendors, local radio stations, and other community members. Let them set up booths at the event. Think outside the box and seek door prizes from local merchants—ask a local wine store to provide a wine-tasting booth, maybe have a pet show contest sponsored by a local vet. Get the idea? Remember to notify the local papers for the credit and PR you will deserve!

Sponsor a Golf Tournament

Like golf? Love publicity? This is a good way to penetrate a niche market. Offer to be a sponsor for a local golf tournament. Get signage, press, and publicity. Take pictures of foursomes on one of the early holes—pictures that you will deliver in person when they are printed! Put them in an attractive folder with your contact information and use them as a door opener to the golfers.

Surveys

Jump-start your cold-calling if you must cold-call by conducting a survey. For example, what are seniors doing about the high cost of prescriptions? Read online www.AARP.com (click on the issues and elections tab) to learn what is of priority concern. Call prospects to help you build your business by having them answer three survey questions. Offer to share the results of the survey. You could include a variety of solutions in the report as well as your information. Make it interesting for prospects to talk with you.

Become a "Warm Up" Act

Find a local professional outside of your industry who offers seminars. LASIK eye surgeons? Plastic surgeons? Hospitals? Dentists? CPAs? Contractors? Connect and offer to do an intro for them—to be a bit of a warm-up act. Try to tie what the professional is promoting in with the need to maximize investment opportunities with you!

Seminars

Later in this publication there are specific ideas on hosting "cheap and easy" seminars that do not require the efforts of a wedding planner to pull off. Seminars that don't take every moment of your time to produce, when done properly are still an excellent way to mass market yourself and your ability!

Finding these prospects isn't enough. You must have a good solid method to track and retain leads. Often a prospect that had no interest or no money when you contacted them will have a different scenario a year or two later. So, always ask if you can return in the future to "touch base" with them.

Stimulated? Don't just sit there worrying; activity will always reward you with success! Make sure you clear any marketing activities you plan to use with your manager and your compliance officers.

Goals and One-page Business Plans

This section should have been first, but I am well aware that the very thought of spending time and energy writing a thirty-page business plan (that may or may not be read) for your manager would send this book into the darkest recess of your desk, never to be opened again!

It may surprise you to know I am with you! A plan should be a living, breathing document that you can view frequently and change as needed. You do need to write your goals, strategies, and the tactics you will use to achieve them, but it should be brief, compelling, and powerful.

Think of a trip you might plan. There are certain details that must be spelled out or you might never arrive at your destination. You must decide where you are going and how long it will take to get there. What mode of transportation will you choose? How much can you afford to invest?

A One-page Plan is the same concept. It must be in writing. I am of the belief that something written becomes a part of your very internal "computer" and somehow you make an unconscious commitment when you scribe your intentions.

What does this One-page Plan stipulate?

Four Steps to a Million:

1. Goals-Business and Personal
2. Strategies and Tactics
3. Reward for Accomplishment
4. Date and Signature

That's it!

Goals—Examples:

- Meet with three appointments every day.
- How much do you plan to generate in gross revenues for the year?
- How much in invested dollars? (This makes a difference regarding product selection—all AUM fee based accounts will require a lot more invested dollars, etc.)
- Break it out by month and attempt to seasonalize it, making sure to consider vacation months and holidays.

- Break it out into weeks and days. How many appointments will you see each day?
- What circumstances will allow you to "reforecast" these goals?
- What do you want to earn (take home) for the year?
- How many new clients would you like to have?
- What new products and services will you learn?
- What new designations or licenses would you like to earn?
- What new things would you like to try?
- Where will you vacation this year?
- What community volunteer or board positions would you like to have?
- And so on—you get the idea.

Okay, now the strategies and the tactics to accomplish the goals are next! A list of twenty marketing ideas preceded this section. Choose three major initiatives to help you accomplish your goals. Three seems to be the best workable number. You can have sub-tactics under each plan, but they should be somehow related to one of the three major initiatives.

To help you accomplish your goals:

- **Strategy** would be: "I am having a seminar a month."
- **Tactics** would be: Choosing: topic, location, venue, wholesaler assistance, PowerPoint, equipment, invitations, etc.
- **Strategy** would be: "I will be doing 'Warm Walking' to local business."
- **Tactics** would be: My message, my personal commercial, my materials to leave with them, my tracking system, deciding which day works best, what follow up methods to use—letter, call, another visit, or a meeting.
- **Strategy** would be: "I am creating a newsletter."
- **Tactics** would be: Choosing the topic, format, canned or personalized, making sure compliance is approved,

frequency of delivery, delivery method (i.e., mail, e-mail, or both), and if you decide to include a photo of yourself.

Last but not Least—Reward for Accomplishment and Signature

This is very important. We all need to see the reward at the end of any endeavor. For some it is more income. For others it is recognition for a job well done. Maybe you are driving a car that is not exactly your dream wheels. Maybe you want to see Italy. Maybe there are several things you will strive for if you hit your goals. Write them down. Putting your "Jane Henry" on the document makes a commitment to yourself.

Give serious thought to this plan. Make sure it is living and breathing, visible always, and changed when strategies need to be adjusted. Break your overall goal into smaller pieces using Time Blocking. List the activities you select so they aren't left to chance.

The very nature of the abbreviated One-page Plan allows you to strike what isn't working and add something else. I promise—some amazing things will happen. It has proven its merit over and over again.

Manage Time with Time Blocking

If you call you doctor with a question, when does he call back? You probably answered—at five o'clock or at the end of the day. Exactly, he controls his time that way.

One of the most overwhelming tasks faced by an advisor is managing time. I know you have heard it all before. Consider the familiar message of blocking time with a new and passionate twist. It is the only workable option proven to accomplish the plethora of tasks and responsibilities that are ancillary to the primary role of a financial advisor, tasks more numerous than ever. Think of time blocking as "making appointments" for activities.

With your number one priority to find people in need of financial guidance, and after a series of interactions to become the provider of that guidance (and hopefully all of the new business that goes along with it), you will need to effectively manage your time.

Time blocking allows the prepared professional to create time for all of the necessary activities—important duties that support, but should never replace the number one priority of closing business. These duties include: marketing, prospecting, planning, learning new products and services, more prospecting, getting additional licenses or designations, more prospecting, correspondence, client service, more prospecting, and community involvement.

There are many options for blocking your time. The basic principal is to write down what needs to be done when and then stick to it. It matters not whether you use ACT, Outlook, Brokers Ally, an old fashioned day planner, a legal pad, or your company's in-house database system. The point is you are in control of your day, your destiny, and your dollars.

If you block time to do research from seven or eight in the morning, for an example, at eight you cease and move on to the next block activity. This allows you to control when you handle problems and return calls. This is especially helpful if you can manage to tend to service issues in one fell swoop at some blocked section of time. Service problems have a way of turning your day upside down.

Too many people live reactively. To be successful as an advisor, one must be relentlessly proactive. By examining daily routines that use blocks of time unconsciously, we find we do this already—we're shopping for groceries, reading the paper, walking the dog, and driving. We eat breakfast in the morning, dinner in the evening, we shower, turn on the news, service the car, pay bills, visit friends, take the kids to school and soccer. All of these activities happen not by chance, but during times we set aside. I suggest that we do this in the same way for our business.

Once you have established the activities in your non-employment life that are "non-negotiable" and are destined to become part of your routine, missing or forgoing them would create stress, havoc, and confusion, right?

You manage to accomplish everything because you know you must in order to keep things in life running smoothly. Everything is inter-related, isn't it? So you do block time, you just aren't fully aware of it.

So, now create the same sense of proactive organization for work. Identify and prioritize the important activities, assign times for these activities, and spend a solid month developing the habit with consistency.

This is also time to eliminate the biggest time-wasters. Reading the *Wall Street Journal* is fine; but do it before you leave the house in the morning. Staring into the computer all day watching up-ticks and down-ticks in the market is just an excuse to avoid productive work unless you are a money manager, and you are most likely not! If you are a smoker, you shave your production to half of what it could be. You lose momentum with frequent breaks, plus you stink when you get back into the smoke-free office. Time-blocking makes you tighten your day and make every moment count.

See the example below for ideas on how to make appointments for your activities! As with life, often the management of time occasionally falls to the wayside. That's okay. But, as with any effort to improve, you pick it right back up the next day. Is it foolproof? Of course not. Life has a way of sending us curves in the form or emergencies and other interruptions. But if you strive to maintain the concept you will be far ahead in the game of managing your time.

A good habit to form is to keep your desk clean of everything but what you are working on at the moment.

By the way, keep office chitchat to a minimum. The folks in your office are usually your competition, trust me. This is a fact of life. The friendliness and the neediest ones will drain your mental resources and often take you off your game.

It may amaze you to know that the guy doing a million now is really no different than you are. He is not smarter or cleverer—he is just committed, focused, and willing to do whatever it takes to hit his goals. He knows it's possible.

"The tougher the fight, the more important the mental attitude."

—Michael Landon (1936–1991)

Sample Time Blocks:

Time Blocks
DATE__________ Make a fresh page for each day

Time: ____To____ Activity__________

Time: ____To______ Activity____________

Dynamic Time For Business
Time: ____To____ Prospect for New Clients - List:________ **SMILE! Use a SCRIPT!**

New prospects: _________

Call back today:
____
____
____

My Main Target Markets!
1. __________________________
2. __________________________
3. __________________________

Notes:

LUNCH/PERSONAL TIME (Move away from desk____To____)
OK to expand time for client meetings or personal business

Time: ____To____ **Activity________________**

Time: ____To____ **Activity** ________________

Time: ____To____ **Activity________________**

Working late? Take a break to be energized and positive~

Evening Calling (twice each week on________&__________)
5:30-7 Prospect for new clients, return calls for working clients, seminars?

Make appointments for your activities, and everyone will profit!

Patti Branco 903-451-9800 www.pattibranco.com

As you can see, it isn't rocket science, it is just a written task list—a "to-do" list, appointments for all that needs to be done. The great thing about time-blocking is that when the time for a certain activity ends, you stop and know it will resume the next day or whenever it is again scheduled! You become proactive rather than reactive.

Learn the R-O-P-E-S:

When juggling tasks these are important areas to keep in mind:

- Referrals
- Opportunity
- Product knowledge and Profiling
- Excellence
- Sales!

Referrals

Referrals are and always have been a key to the advisor's business development. Your existing clients are the most likely source of referrals, yet study after study reminds us that this is the last place we look for new business.

Several years ago a fund company did a formal study. Approximately seventy-five percent of clients surveyed said they would recommend their financial advisor to a friend or family member. The kicker? Of that group willing to recommend their advisor to a friend or family member, only a small percentage were ever asked to do so!

Advisors often say that they forget or just can't seem to get into the habit of asking for referrals. Some say they feel it is beneath them, akin to groveling. Others feel as though they are begging. Some just don't have the right script!

What do clients say about all this? First, when they are happy with the service they receive, the majority would gladly refer to their advisor, if asked. Whatever the underlying cause or reason for not receiving referrals from existing and satisfied clients, this is an important area to consider more carefully.

Many brokers have come up with clever ways of fostering a healthy referral business, the cleverest being a wirehouse broker who kept a stack of Tiffany wine glasses on his credenza. When clients saw that popular little aqua gift box they would ask what they were for.

"Oh," the savvy broker would say, "those are the gifts I give as a thank you when a client gives me a qualified referral." What do you think the client is thinking of now? He would add the word "qualified" to encourage the client to submit a *valid* referral and not someone seeking budget guidance or help with credit card debt or an existing client gaming the system. This Tiffany wine glass broker got about fifty percent of his new business from referrals alone. Then when he sends or delivers one of these thank-you gifts, he includes a note that simply says, "Thanks so much for referring your friend Mr. Jones; I appreciate your vote of confidence. Enjoy this small token of my gratitude, and I hope to help you complete the set!"

Today expensive wine glasses may be out of reach because of affordability and NASD gifting restrictions, but the idea could be used with anything collectable from any other store. With Internet shopping, something even more unique could be discovered from the plentiful sources available around the globe. Of course, your manager must approve any marketing plan and there are annual limits on gift values, so know the facts before you get creative.

Other good referral tips: give every new client two cards, one for them and "one for a friend." Send out quarterly news letters or postcards mentioning referrals along with other business, as a 'by the way'. Hold a client appreciation dinner for the top clients and make their entry fee a requirement to bring a friend along. Be consistent and shameless in your promotion as that is the key to receiving referrals.

Opportunity

Opportunity knocks, and is often ignored. Learn how to hear the knock. Learn how to find it, recognize it, and how to harvest it. Plan and think creatively. Networking, volunteering, partnerships, board positions all yield opportunity and referrals. Never judge someone by clothing or the car he or she drives. You may miss an opportunity. Tell everyone you meet what you do and the benefits you provide.

I once knew a single client, a very wealthy business man, who owned a Silver Cloud Rolls Royce. However, when he had a date with someone new that he liked, he borrowed his parents old Ford and dressed down because he didn't want someone who might be more interested in his money than in him. He probably appeared much the same way as a non-qualified prospect might! Keep your radar on and your judgment off.

Product Knowledge

Take this simple test: If you can't describe a common stock, a preferred stock, a bond, a mutual fund, a REIT, an option, a unit investment trust, a wrap account, a managed money account, a variable annuity, a fixed annuity, and if you don't have at least a basic understanding of the many hybrid investments like spiders and ETFs, then you'd better get back to the book because you are heading for trouble!

Complete and total understanding of all the products and services available is the most under utilized set of tools advisors have at their disposal. So many advisors aim to specialize or to choose the products that appeal to them or get stuck on the first one that proves successful or the hot product of the day. They leave so much business on the proverbial table.

Lack of broad product knowledge always puzzles me because this is the easiest part of the equation. But here is what happens: A young broker decides that stocks are sexy and annuities are stupid. So, new broker dives into stocks and pays no attention to anything else. Or a rookie gets a huge sale with preferred stocks and suddenly, that is the main focus. This is akin to a contractor showing up to build a house with only a hammer or a saw!

Investment products are the tools of the advisor, and if you want to at least "attract" enough clients to be successful, then you'd better invest the time and learn what your "tools" are and how they work! You also have to understand what they currently hold in order to discuss intelligently.

Sure you can specialize, but even top medical specialists have to learn basic medicine before becoming a specialist! By the way, if you have the knowledge and experience to specialize, proclaiming you are a "specialist" for seniors or retirees or doctors or another area of investors really needs to be backed up with solid knowledge of that group's particular requirements, issues, and desires as well as any required licenses. For example, most recent ruling states you need a Series 65 or a 66 license to even mention the word "planning."

Seniors? You should be reading AARP and learning all the important hot issues. They may be different than you think with the Baby Boomer generation. Doctors? Subscribe to a medical magazine and be aware that malpractice insurance is a drain on their resources. It goes on long after they are retired. You get the idea—use your learning as a way of finding the opportunity to discuss your research with the very same professionals you wish to work with!

Please become familiar with your tools and how they fit your clients' objectives. These are the solutions to their problems. Hate those boring annuities? Well, thirty percent of all bank clients own a fixed annuity. Think a variable annuity is for the sissies? According to LIMRA and current Industry Statistics (LIMRA):

- 2006: $236.2 billion in total annuity sales
  - Up 9% over 2005
  - A record
- 2006: Fixed Annuity sales-$75.6 billion
  - Down 5% over 2005
- 2006: Variable Annuity sales-$160.6 billion
  - Up 17% over 2005

In contrast, during the year 2000, $23 billion went in to annuities and the rumor was that they were falling from favor. Thought provoking? Maybe this is worth considering as part of your tool chest.

We all know lotteries use annuities if someone selects life payout. A little known fact is that creative use of fixed annuities can help a doctor deal in advance with the lifelong payments on his malpractice insurance. Annuities are also used in structured insurance settlements where someone with little or no experience managing money wins the award in the form of a predestined lifelong stream of income. However, the simplest, most common use is for deferring the annual taxes until withdrawn and the opportunity to name a beneficiary and avoid probate. They are not sexy, but they are popular.

Many brokers have told me they want to keep their clients' money liquid and available for good investment opportunities.

Fine, say I, for a portion of it. But no matter what *you* want, investors always have a portion of their assets in long-term vehicles. Wake up, and don't be afraid to tie up! There are many levels to the investment pyramid.

It isn't about you, or what your firm would like to see as the core product offering. It is about your clients, what they need, and what they are familiar with. Before you hop on the managed money for fee sale, or offer everyone those corporate bonds that you like so much, or toss a mutual fund prospectus on the table, learn to ask the right questions and understand the client's existing financial situation.

Profiling Techniques from Scotland Yard

Whether you are selling a gardening tool or a financial plan, the whole premise of selling is based on knowing what the client needs and wants.

Missing this part of the puzzle creates a serious deficiency in the successful launch of an advisor's career. This competency—the ability to interview and profile effectively—takes confidence and skill, but both can be easily acquired through learning, scripting, and practice. So often a broker jumps into the sales process before gathering enough information to make a recommendation that will result in a sale, and moreover, a lasting relationship.

Imagine going to the doctor with a sore ankle and the first thing out of his mouth is, "Here is a prescription. This will fix that ankle right up."

Another risk of "shooting from the hip" is that you have a very small chance of hitting the right match. You may get a sale but you won't win the relationship. To get to the million dollar mark you're going to need deep and lasting relationships where you are viewed as the "go-to" guy or gal to use as a resource for every financial reason.

It doesn't require a whole complete two-hour financial plan to ask some basic questions—questions that can make all the difference in the end result—such as:

- What are your goals?
  —What do you want this money to do?
- What is your age?
  —How young are you?
- Risk tolerance?
  —On a scale of one to ten with one being absolutely no risk to ten being speculative, where are you? (Most people answer five.)
- Tax situation?
  —Are you paying your favorite "uncle" too much?
- Investment experience
  —Tell me about you investment experience.
- What amount do you keep in fixed accounts and what rate is the return?
- What experience have you had with investments other than these cash accounts?
- What has worked well?
- What was your biggest disappointment?
- What's important to you regarding your money?
  —Whatever the answer, continue with, "What's most important about that?" to get to the root of the problem.

> In case you are interrupted with "Why?" answer honestly by saying something like, "I would like to get a snapshot of your financial picture before I discuss any other investments!" Now you become the hero.

G.R.E.A.T.S

If you are on the fly—in the car or approached at a party—a quick acronym to remember is G.R.E.A.T.S. Perhaps you're new and must learn how to begin probing. Before the advent of technology, G.R.E.A.T.S was a profiling tool I created that generated a lot of revenue. I call it my low-tech profiling system. If you are away from your desk or approached in a social setting this allows you to gather and converse without the benefit of your legal pad. Of course, script the questions so they are in your own words and you become comfortable with them. Press on—these are things you must know before making a suitable recommendation.

Here is the acronym spelled out and defined:

G—Goals

"Mr. Client, What are your goals for your money?"
Sometimes they need help, so a follow question I like is with, "When do you plan to spend it?"

R—Resources

What does the client have and where is it?
"Please tell me about other CDs and investments you may have."

This can take some time if they have a lot of money. Just keep saying, "Anything else you can think of?" Gather. Write each down in a list unless you are unable to at that particular time.

E—Experience

This is often a deal saver! "Please tell me your best experience with investing and your least favorite." Make it conversational. You will learn a lot about the prospect.

A—Age and Anticipated time frame

"How young are you today?"
"When will you need your liquid money? Any major purchases on the horizon? Any emergency vacations planned?"

Get the idea?

T—Taxes

At this point you may be able to comment on the fact that the client has given a lot of consideration to taxes, based on his or her responses to R (resources) and E (experience) or it might still be a question, "Do you feel you are paying too much income tax to your favorite Uncle—Sam?"

S—Safety

Finally, the last thing you want to do is have an hour discussion about investments only to hear, "Oh, these aren't insured?" Being upfront is the way to get past that potential obstacle of someone wanting absolutely no risk by pointing out the nature and potential risk of investments. Say something like, "Mr. Client, I see you have a lot of CDs. The solutions I will discuss with you in order to generate more income, (save taxes, diversify, look for growth] are not federally insured. Are you okay with that?" If needed, a reasonable analogy is that a client's house and property goes up and down in value. This is usually the biggest investment the client has!

For a client with extensive investment experience this last question is not critical unless your firm requires it because many bank programs do look for that extra assurance of understanding. Most new account forms mention risk. The experienced investor already understands that without any market risk there is risk in losing purchasing power and the importance of staying ahead of inflation. It is still wise to cover those bases and keep good notes that risk tolerance was discussed.

By now you should have all the information you need to either proceed with a more elaborate assessment plan or to make a suitable recommendation based on the client's experience and sophistication.

When a client discloses different investments owned, have enjoyed or have hated, you will have an enhanced level of self-confidence with a full knowledge of those products and services. And don't ever assume you know it all, or have it all.

A True Story

Consider the story of Debbie S. who felt that there wasn't much need to utilize the computerized financial plan her company was touting for their clients. She enjoyed her winning legal pad approach. She was finally convinced to participate and decided to try using this simple profiling tool on existing clients that she knew had no more money to invest. In her estimation, they were the safe ones to approach.

She felt comfortable asking the certain clients to allow her to "practice" this computerized plan with them and amid giggles and some serious curiosity she got pretty good at entering data and understanding the reports.

On the fifth client practice session she entered information with the client's input and the result popped up that the client would have to add $6,000 per month in order to retire when and how she had selected for the questionnaire. Debbie knew this small business owner with a local food stand had already invested everything with her and that she certainly did not have that kind of money. Imagine Debbie's face when the client asked if she should bring the check for $6,000 to the branch or mail it in monthly!

Someone reading this book who isn't in the financial services environment might think we are out in left field and think that surely all licensed advisors have this down! Aren't they trained about this? But advisors who know better are smiling because I hit a nerve.

Know your products. Know your services. Don't stop learning the first time you enjoy a 25K month. Have your favorite products but don't force feed them to clients. Wait until you have the required information before recommending a product or service, and then select from a full range of suitable and available investments.

Be the Expert

Own the entire relationship, creating an atmosphere where the client will come to you or your firm for every possible financial need. This is the heart and soul of building truly full-service client relationships—the modern goal of most firms.

Excellence, family, and fitness!

Become the "Best in the Business." You can be the guy with the Silver Cloud or the gal building a million-dollar beach house.

Excellence can be cultivated. Being the best that you can be and gaining prominence in the financial industry circles relies on that triumph. Striving for the highest level of success comes with the admonition to maintain a strong balance with work, rest, and family.

I want to emphasize the importance of establishing your boundaries early. Being the best you can be is not about time invested; but rather, the *quality* of time invested, so be certain to give equal weight to life, family, and work.

One weak area in the equation and the other areas will suffer. The very reason you go to work is as important as the work itself—your family, sports, your life outside of work, your volunteer work, whatever it may be.

Excellence also goes hand-in-hand with integrity, always taking the high road at all costs. The best way to ensure integrity is to remember that "perception is reality." If it looks even slightly like a conflict of interest, it probably is.

Anatomy of a Sale

Sales, dissected into stages: We can call "sales" whatever we want in an attempt to legitimatize the process, but it is still selling, and it is still the basis for the most profitable industry known to mankind.

You can't leave a McDonald's or the local grocery store without an attempted additional sale by the clerk who is trained to ask, "Fry's with that?" or at the grocer's, "Did you find everything you wanted?" The shoe salesman wants you to purchase shoe cleaner, the car salesman has a special on satellite radio, and the computer store wants to sell you replacement insurance for your equipment purchase. These tag lines and many others add millions in revenue to the companies—sales.

There are distinct phases of the sales process and learning how to work with them will reward you with a success.

Stage One is the attraction stage. Be it on the phone, in person, or through the U.S. mail, if you have won the interest of a qualified prospect, the sales process has begun. The person is open to connecting with you. It is now in your hands.

Stage Two is the phase where you learn what your clients need. Win the client's confidence and trust, because you are competent, confident, and sporting "excellence"! The client is now comfortable enough to give you all the information you require to do business with him or her. This is a warm-up that you must control.

Stage Three is where you interview the client and learn all that you need to know to make suitable recommendations about the next step. Unfortunately this is often skipped or shortened for a variety of reasons, usually the wrong ones.

Stage Four is the "close." It could be introductions to other services (i.e., financial or estate planning or insurance) or it could be the real *close*—preferably the opening of a new account.

Ideally all stages can take place in one sitting! The four stages can occur in a quick minute or over a period of time. At the end of each stage and the onset of the next you must learn to do it with grace and firmness—a "let's get down to business" transition that you have prepared.

Lastly, if it is time to close, you close. Your close could be a referral to another department. It might be another appointment to continue the process. It could be an opening of an account. Basically, it is asking the client to take action, here and now.

Not a qualified prospect? At the very least, it might be the mere admonishment to keep a meager amount of money liquid for emergencies with a prospect that really wasn't qualified to invest after all! When the client does have funds, that client will seek you out.

Note that a lot of professional reps get caught up in the second and third stage of sales and never get out of those stages into stage four. It may be lack confidence in their product knowledge. Sometimes it is fear of failing or being rejected. It is often because they like the sound of their own voice.

Sometimes they try to over convince the prospect of their talent and skill. They begin to bore them or at least confuse them. So if you are an overly analytical conversationalist, zip it and become a better listener. Remember, the prospect is there for his or her own needs.

I recently observed a rep in a social setting during lunch. Conversation flowed across and around the table of eight. The rep just looked left and right constantly waiting for an opportunity to jump in. He didn't even hear what anyone else was saying, and every statement he made was about himself, his connections, or his family. Ugly.

It is about them, not you. Imaging going to a doctor for an ailment and the doc bending your ear about himself. You sit there just waiting to tell him about your tennis elbow and maybe a couple other items but when it is your turn, the doc seems less interested. How frustrating. Is that your style?

Active listening involves a focus, a concerned posture, rapt and sincere attention, nodding acknowledgement, hearing, and the observation of body language. It's very different from waiting for someone to stop speaking so you can jump in there. Relax—enjoy and listen to your prospects—often you can learn a lot from the experience.

Never answer your cell phone or your office phone while in a client meeting unless the call is expected and pertaining to their situation! It is in bad taste, and reduces your chance to connect with that client. During a meal or in another public place this is even more important.

Attract, Build Trust, Profile, Close

A broker asked me once, with a look of disbelief, "Do you think it is ever appropriate to close a sale at the first appointment?" My answer was in the form of a few questions:

- Tell me what you do when a prospect comes in with a rollover check that is three days away from a taxable event.

- What would you do if a prospect says he or she has been meaning to invest this nest egg for over a year, had little time, and the person is now in front of you?
- What if it is to establish a simple college fund for a gift?
- My answer? Yes! Of course there are times it is appropriate to close during the first meeting—times when "let's mull this over" doesn't cut it—and it is your job to determine when that is a legitimate way to begin opening an account. If there is a clear need present, start the paperwork and begin the relationship.

After the First Sale

The main goal is to always turn the initial sale into a long-term relationship, not merely a one-time transaction. If you do open an account during the first meeting, make sure you set a second appointment to address other concerns clients may have and to go over their first statement to ensure understanding.

Develop a "follow-up" activity that instills loyalty and generates referrals. This includes handwritten thank-you notes and proactive communication with your client. Have a tickler file and invite your clients back at regular intervals for a review. You can even set the date for the next meeting before they leave, just as the dentist does.

Think about the last thing you purchased and what motivated the sale. Emotion? Maybe it was about the benefits of the item of your desire. Always remember, benefits sell—not features, not price, benefits. Snazzy new car? The benefits of transportation, good mileage, prestige outweigh the other important notables. That big screen television for your media room—the benefit of the viewing pleasure outweighs all the features. When you go to an outrageously expensive restaurant, what is the benefit? The benefits of investing are more income, tax advantages, and a solid retirement. Enjoying your personality and high quality service may also be a benefit.

Of course you need to fully disclose important features and risks and explain the investment you may be recommending; just remember to point out the benefits to owning this investment.

Develop scripts for every step of the process and then learn the scripts until they become natural. (There is more about this in another section on scripting.)

Speak Their Language—No Buzzwords!

Most brain surgeons don't fully understand currency risk, yield curves, and portfolio rebalancing, hedge funds or variable annuities any more than you would understand their medical terms! But everyone understands that money from other countries can be unpredictable and risky. Everyone knows what it means to make sure all of his or her retirement nest egg isn't in one basket. Most people "get it" if they are going to get a check every month or have the opportunity to name a beneficiary, defer taxes, and will earn more than a CD. Make simple explanations, no jargon.

People usually seek the three things I named as benefits: more income, tax advantages, and growth for retirement. Sometimes they want a combination of all three. From new saver to wealthy senior, you will find the threads of these three requirements in every situation.

Don't Quit—There are Solutions to Each Challenge

There is a lot of competition in the financial services industry. With the terribly high washout rate it is easy to get discouraged. But for those who figure it all out, there is a new world waiting on the other side of success. Think about it and go for the gold!

True Story: I will share the story of "Sam," affectionately known as the "Kid." In a team with three others "Sams," he snagged that nickname. Hired with little experience and almost no understanding of financial products, he won a small spot because he called every day to see if the job had been filled; hiring him was the only way to get him to stop calling. I kept thinking if he uses that kind of follow-up we may have a winner on our hands.

He had gotten a license from a license mill and had worked as a cashier for a major wirehouse firm for six months. He proudly answered my question about his level of investment experience by telling me he researched and bought a mutual fund for his girlfriend.

Sam's frequent calls became the topic of the day. My entire office staff knew him. My supervisor said, "Give him a chance. Your instincts are good. Create something for him, train him, and keep him on a short leash."

We did. He agreed to be "like a sponge," allowing us to mold him and fill him with our experience and wisdom. In this successful bank investment program he shadowed our best reps and was soon ready to take on the world.

He tripled production in a region that was deemed to go nowhere. This was in the mid-nineties. He broke records in the program, blew away the brokers who had been there for years, and always did the right thing for the client. Sam was (and I am sure still is) a very high producer, doing well over five hundred gross commissions every year. Why not more? Because he was content to settle at that level which left a little more time for golf!

To this day Sam thanks this author and says he owes me his success. "Not true!" I tell him, "I opened the door for you and you ran through." I have opened a lot of doors for people and I only witnessed one like Sam. Carpe diem—seize the day—and every precious moment in it.

As I mentioned before, Sam is not his real name. This story is an example of someone who saw the vision of success and was open to doing everything required to make it happen. His secret? He left his ego at the door.

Is it Time for an Assistant?

At some time on your path to million dollar production you will consider the benefits of having an assistant. There are as many ways to view and to fund this process are there are investment products.

When you hit a certain level, many firms will give you "part" of an assistant's time. You and several others will share one person paid for by your company. Often the amount of assistant hours relegated to you will depend on your level of production. It's been my experience that the magic number for scoring the services of a shared assistant is usually somewhere between two hundred fifty thousand and five hundred thousand gross. Sometimes you are allowed to contribute a bonus based on your production if the assistant is also licensed. If the assistant is not licensed it is a general rule that they cannot participate in your commissions.

To earn the services of a full-time assistant dedicated to you and you alone, you need to be in the million dollar production range or be willing to pay a good portion of the salary yourself.

Keep in mind, it takes money to make money, as in any enterprise. If you are on an upward thrust, effectively engaging assistance in some form, even if your firm does not sponsor helpers as is the case with most independents, it might be worthwhile to make an investment in your future.

I frequently see talented assistants being used as secretaries, fluffing up the ego of the registered rep. The RR moves some of the administrative work over to the assistant and nothing really occurs to add additional revenue. This is a major mistake if you are looking for that next level.

I recently met a broker who says he would never use his assistant as a secretary. He feels that he is the one that needs to be familiar with anything regarding his operation and paperwork flow "What about error corrections," I asked. "Does the assistant take care of those?"

"No," he clarified. "If I made an error, I owe the client an apology and I take care if it myself. The assistant is there to help me build my business."

The assistant is there to help him get more sales opportunities, not to give him more time for long lunches and mid-week golf games.

To get the most from the services of an assistant you should build a job description that grows your business. The position should be aimed at developing business, lining up appointments, and deepening existing relationships. Having a licensed assistant is preferable, as he or she can write business, but non-licensed assistants can be utilized effectively as well. Daily activities should never be left to chance.

Professional titles are important as well. I dislike the tone of "sales assistant" (clients don't like being "sold"). I strive to see more titles such as: Client Services Manager, Investment Associate, Director of Client Services, Registered Associate, Team Member. You get the idea.

Choose Your Assistant Carefully

It may take some time to find the best candidate. Never settle when it comes to this important role on your path to success. Hiring the wrong person may actually hurt your efforts rather than help, and getting rid of that person in this litigious and overly regulated day and age is like moving a mountain. Make sure you check references. Since folks are hard to reach, I ask for five, saying I may call three. Then I call all of them! If you see any inconsistencies or outright fabrication, file the application in the circular file—the trash. Don't let impatience fuel denial and cause you to overlook a glaring shortcoming that will only get worse.

Checklist for hiring the right assistant:

- Licensed
- Experience with administrative work
- Outgoing personality
- A fit with the existing culture
- Positive
- Ambitious
- Desire to learn and be mentored
- Reliable
- High energy
- Geographically desirable
- Good transportation
- No history of job-hopping

I hate to mention this because it is a sensitive subject, but when I see piercing and other body art, I wonder what a client will think. Make sure your selection fits the culture and that your employment agreement has a ninety-day probation period in case you erred in your choice. If you're hiring an assistant for a rock band, body art is cool! Otherwise, nix it.

I once hired an assistant for the president of a large investment program, with reps in dozens of branches. She came to three interviews dressed to the nines, suited, classy. On her first day of work she wore a micro mini, black tights, and a halter top! When I approached the subject of the drastic change, trying to be delicate because this was her first week and I liked her background, she answered, "Oh, the suits? Those were my mom's!" Well, thankfully, it resolved itself and she accepted the need for business attire in the office, but it was a wake-up call for me to bring the topic of professional attire into the interview, and not to assume anything.

Aligning Your Values

What is your reason for being in this business? So many bright young graduates and successful career "changers" enter this field with an eye on potential earnings. If the motive is only to get rich, you may never hit the goals you desire. I challenge you to review and evaluate your reasons for entering the business of selling investments, to research the firm you are considering, and to identify early on (along with your values), your own personal and professional strengths. If money is the only factor, you will never get to second base without trials and many tribulations.

Ask yourself, "What are the character traits and values that make up the fabric of who I am?" With careful introspection comes self-awareness and wisdom. Learn the firm's attitude toward volunteerism and family priorities. Find out what hours you are expected to keep, what marketing assistance is available, and if there is much travel. Make sure you feel similarly, as this will help you formulate a personal mission statement with respect and loyalty for the right firm.

You need to have your ethics compass in place to deal with the challenge of living up to the highest personal and professional standards in this profession. You certainly need to like people, be willing to take the high road in all circumstances, and have a bit of a servant's heart.

Many important issues are usually not covered in initial training classes; instead they are buried in the volumes of new-hire training materials, and often left to chance. Therefore you need to do a little research on your own before signing on.

This can be an extremely difficult task at times, but making sure you are a good fit and that this is a place you would like to be is rewarding in the long-run.

Confidence with Class

Class is like the wind—you know it when you feel it but it is hard to describe! Confidence with class is a winning combination that combines your knowledge, skills, and "dress for success" image. Possessing one without the other will impede your progress. Unfortunately, people still judge the package first, the content later.

Confidence can be gained through knowledge. Persistent study and research will increase your understanding of investment choices and allow you to offer them appropriately to clients. Utilize wholesalers, company sponsored training events, and a systematic method of self-study to become a virtual walking encyclopedia of investments. Network with the top person in your office. Eavesdrop. It's acceptable to "steal" with your eyes and ears. Seek a mentor and offer to do some of their grunt work in exchange for the opportunity to hang around and observe their methods.

Class and refinement are required to match the affluence of the clients you wish to acquire. Image, manners, and old-fashioned courtesy are all important on the way to million dollar production. If you haven't mastered courtesy on the way to adulthood, make it a point to learn it now.

- Open doors for others

- Always say please and thank you
- Use Mr. and Mrs. when addressing elders unless they suggest otherwise
- Hello trumps "Hi"
- Make sure your grammar is correct
- Go easy on wearing fragrances
- Always ask for permission to "probe"
- Always speak slowly and clearly, especially when using the phone
- Be a dynamic listener
- Return phone calls to *everyone*

Dressing and acting like the affluent client you are seeking will put you ahead of the game. Learn how to walk the walk, talk the talk, and run the race but without sacrificing your own values and personal style. You can accomplish this without a fancy pedigree or a million dollars in the bank.

Wear conservative suits, clean and pressed always. Even if you can only afford two suits in the beginning, create more pizzazz with shirts, ties, and pocket handkerchiefs. Invest in a luxurious briefcase. When you are told it is casual day, beware. It is still best to have the total professional image; but if you must partake, make it a classy polo or an open collar dress shirt and nice slacks, never jeans. With your luck, casual day will be the day the billionaire you have been tracking shows up and your confidence will fly out the window if you don't feel and look professional. Corporate casual days are falling to the wayside as they have become corporate sloppily dressed days.

> Once "David" (not his real name) came to work with a suit and only the front of his shirt ironed. The air conditioning broke down in the middle of a very hot summer and forgetting that he hadn't ironed the whole shirt he took his jacket off. It was a pretty embarrassing experience!

Confidence and class are definitely requirements for the million dollar producer!

Let your "Handshake" Show Strength

Pay attention to how you shake hands with someone and make sure it is firm, not too firm, and professional. This ritual is an important first impression that you make at the onset of the relationship. Men and ladies, grasp the others hand 'web-to-web' and clasp your hand firmly around the other persons hand. There is nothing worse the a gentle wiggly, and sometimes clammy, handshake with no substance to it!

If you push your hand forward until the web between the thumb and forefinger of your hand connect with the web and forefinger of the other, it is usually a good handshake.

Effective Script Writing—The Importance of Words

Think about the last great movie you've seen and how your attention was absorbed to the point of total focus. Maybe the background music danced in your memory for days. That is what a "script" is all about.

We all take in a movie occasionally and pay ten bucks or more to see our favorite star. We laugh or cry, but it doesn't change the fact that we are hypnotized as they are reading from a memorized script!

Now that puts scripting into a different prospective, doesn't it? The point is to encourage you to know what you are going to say before you say it and to say it naturally, confidently, and sincerely using a prepared script.

A successful advisor will develop an effective script, become comfortable with it, and make adjustments as he or she goes, keeping what works and changing what doesn't.

Below are a few sample ideas for scripts, which are a fairly common commodity in our industry. What will be unique about this advice regarding scripting is the encouragement to make them your own words! Write, build, test, and revise your own personalized scripts—I can't tell you exactly what to say!

Using a scripted greeting works well with everyone you meet, everywhere you go, with every hand you shake. Unlock opportunity by asking what others do for a living, and it will usually be followed by the opportunity to say what you do! Be prepared—don't wing it. Replying about what you do should be a carefully crafted script, compelling and laden with benefits for the recipient, delicately offering the opportunity to do business.

Let's craft one now—a thirty-second "personal commercial" for you to use with someone you meet in the elevator or on the golf course. Of course you can say the entire answer; I broke it out to make a point:

Who are you?

(This should be your name and your title—period.)

"Hello, I'm Patti Branco."

Where do you work?

(Your firm and floor if it in your office building.)

"I am an advisor up on thirty at Best Brokerage and Insurance."

What do you offer to me [benefits]?

This is where people go wrong. They give a long dissertation about their ability to manage wealth and how bright and well educated they are. Yes this is important, but this short opportunity to introduce your services must convey benefits!

Example of a compelling answer: "I help clients earn more income, plan for retirement, and save on taxes." ("Wow," the prospect thinks, "I need you!")

Why would I want to meet with you?

Same answer as above.

Okay, how difficult is this?

Who are you?

"Hello, I'm Patti Branco"

"I am an advisor up on 30 at Best Brokerage and Insurance."

What do you do? (What do you offer to me? [Benefits])

"I help clients earn more income, plan for retirement, and save on taxes."

Now write your own thirty-second personal commercial for someone you meet in the elevator and when time is short. Of course you can say the entire answer and engage in conversation, depending on the time involved. I broke it out to make a point. Remember to smile. Open the conversation by asking the person about himself or herself...

Who are you?

____

Where do you work?

____

What do you offer to me (benefits)?

____

____

____

____

____

Think about your best sales presentation, your effective profiling technique, and your close. Capture each on paper so you can refine it and capture the points that worked well; eliminate the things that didn't. Words are important.

Make your scripts like the best movies—the ones that move people to emotion and action; impress them with your professionalism. Don't leave the most important dialogue to chance!

Practice. Tape yourself and make sure your voice is clear and strong. Make sure you are articulate and don't roll words together. Enunciate. Don't talk in a monotone. If you can, videotape and judge your action like the professional sports folks do!

Managing Your Manager

This topic is not discussed very often. It is about some of the secret and sacred activities regarding the management, motivation, and occasional disposal of non-productive advisors.

Never is it more clear how important the activity of "sales" becomes, and how easily the high washout rate is accepted across the board as a routine business custom.

The brokerage industry and the world of financial services is a competitive and emotionally charged environment at best. The sooner you learn to "manage" yourself, the better off you will be.

Many new brokers seal their fate early by beginning the relationship with their manager in an incorrect way. They seek constant approval and disregard the fact that the branch manager has numerous management responsibilities. Inadvertently, new brokers become a nuisance. They are often perceived as too needy.

Other times they become the branch busybody—always meddling and gossiping at the water cooler. They are going to "fix" the world around them . . . and their way is the best way. If this rings true to you, stop. Steer clear and MYOB.

You must learn to effectively establish your identity, self-promote your successes, and stay out of the everyday limelight! Rookies vie for the attention of the boss. They want the recognition they often deserve for a job well done or an extraordinary successful month. That is human nature. However, with the positive reinforcement sought there is often the risk of being in the spotlight during the times you would prefer a low profile.

One of my least favorite expressions has been "hero to zero" because sad but true is the fact that the broker usually represents a number to that manager. If the broker misses these subtle but salient points, he or she can be doomed from the start. Forget lame excuses for lack of production, the manager has heard it all. It doesn't matter that you are a seminar maven, a computer whiz, a nice guy, had major surgery, tend a sick parent, or are a great example to others. Hero to zero—no gross, no respect.

A good manager always has a pipeline of candidates waiting to take your place. You are looking for prospects; he is on the lookout for talent. He is judged on his ability to recruit.

Another manager relationship pitfall is the "friendly manager" game. Often somewhat paranoid, the manager wants information from the floor and he or she befriends you in order to learn what is happening with the team. In order to win your confidence the friendly manager will share things with you that are confidential, sometimes even personal. Then, when the risk of having done so becomes apparent to the manager's sensibility, he or she will drop your alliance like a hot potato, maybe even hope to see you exit.

On the other end of the spectrum, perhaps you become truly best friends with the branch manger. Then the manager leaves or is transferred. Will the new replacement see you as a threat—part of the old guard?

The bottom line is that being low key is best. Do your work, keep your head down, and allow the reward for being excellent to be a nice fat paycheck and satisfied clients.

If you are reading this book you might leave a copy for your manager. There is a section on leadership written just for managers!

Being a Team Player

Trite and often overused, the team-player concept is still a valid stepping-stone for the successful broker and one of the best ways to win the favor of your manager without being a pest.

There is strength in unity and in numbers. That was sure obvious in 2001 when our beautiful nation was attacked by rabid, deranged terrorists. America pulled together as never before. The power of a group united for the same cause is the most powerful force in the world. Churches, organizations like the Red Cross, and others, even trade unions, showed the positive result of joining forces.

Working with others in an unselfish and open fashion will increase your odds of success. If there are fifty other brokers in your office and you were all able to share ideas and information, you would really be able to maximize your efforts. Can you imagine that?

How? You can orchestrate a consortium to have brainstorming sessions regularly because even in a casual fashion, sharing and helping each other can only help everyone involved. Become a team leader.

Professional speakers call this a mastermind group. Once a week have everyone meet for an early breakfast. Have a topic of the week and let everyone share his or her success stories and ideas. Allow members to bounce ideas off the group. Give the group a successful sounding team name and make sure it doesn't turn into a gripe session! Rotate different coordinators responsible for an agenda and to arrange the meeting location.

Examples of successful business groups that meet for the purpose of business development and performance improvement include: Toastmasters International, Business Networking International (BNI), Chambers of Commerce, the National Speakers Association and many others available if you do a little research.

Politically Correct

We are all Americans and we come in a variety of sizes, colors, and ethnic origins. Not only is it illegal and mean-spirited to malign someone who is different, it is a recipe for failure.

There is never room in any professional environment for jokes about race, creed, religion, or sexual preference. Unwelcome stalking by a smitten coworker toward another is grounds for dismissal. Suggestive jokes and swearing can get you fired, especially if someone lodges a complaint. Learn how to navigate the gray areas of water-cooler talk and avoid the troublemakers.

Illegal activities in these areas are grounds for termination because they are costly and have landed many firms into unwanted litigation and disruptive arbitrations. Most firms feel that if you have been called on these issues once, it is bound to happen again and prefer to remove the problem.

Most of this is common sense, so avoid problems by maintaining your class, integrity, and confidence. Stay away from others who engage in such discourse. This is not the place for a million dollar producer. Besides, unconstructive thinking usually impedes progress. As you thinketh so you are.

Often employees think the above mentioned rules are grist for the management mill having no impact on them as employees. Wrong. It is usually spelled out in your employment manual and sometimes in your rep agreement. Employees are expected to adhere to the same standards when it comes to basic HR policies designed to follow federal requirements.

Compliance is Protection

Everyone abhors compliance. The advisor usually views compliance as the evildoer or the deal killer. To be successful you must view compliance as your partner. Compliance is there to protect you and the firm by ensuring work is done properly. Your E&O insurance, like any insurance policy, covers you *only* as long as you are operating within the law. Work efficiently with your compliance officer to remove roadblocks and make sure you are protected from a disgruntled client who wants to clean your clock.

A simple effusive thank-you note from a new and overly enthusiastic advisor promising, "that your new funds will make you wealthy," can show up long after the thrill of the new account is gone, when in fact they have failed to perform, and are now the subject of a formal dispute.

Give the compliance team a break. If they are over the top let the branch manager straighten things out for the office.

Managers know the value of good compliance and can also recognize if the compliance team is anti-sales, or out of bounds. This is rare, but it happens occasionally. So keep cool and let management do its job.

Avoid Arbitration

I have been an NASD Arbitrator since the mid-nineties. My opinion of arbitration is that it is the most fair and one of the finest ways to resolve disputes between clients and advisors, advisors and firm disputes, and advisor-to-advisor disputes. NASD members and the investing public can arbitrate unresolved issues and any issue related to the investment business, contracts, employment within our industry, and complaints. The panel can consist of a panel of your peers (usually three arbitrators, and often one arbitrator for smaller cases under 25K) and the process is more relaxed than a courtroom proceeding.

In arbitration, the rules and technicalities used in a court of law are important to an extent, but the main goal is to get to the truth. That often means allowing both parties to be heard without objection.

Everything your compliance department does in the way of restriction or documentation is a way to protect you, create an accurate record, and make sure the appropriate recommendations are made. If you end up in arbitration you will have a good bargaining position with good documentation, accurate notes, and operationally complete files.

Do you realize that the new account form is a contract between you and the client? You are signing that contract on behalf of your firm. The firm has delegated that responsibility to you by accepting you and your licenses. If new account paperwork is missing information or has erroneous information or if information on your copy is different from the client's copy, and a dispute arises, you lose. If the client calls you to task with a change of heart regarding an investment you recommended, the client gets what the client wants, usually, if there is not a valid contract, aka (also known as) the new account form!

This topic is so often minimized because it is distasteful. No matter how terrific you are, even as the company's top rep, if you take shortcuts you can fall under the truck of compliance. Just do it right, don't cut corners, and don't take compliance guidance personally! It is there to help you and your firm avoid problems.

Be aware also that every compliance chief interprets the rules according to his or her understanding, and from firm to firm the requirements can vary. If you switch firms you cannot rewrite the rules for your new firm according to what you were used to before.

A good compliance officer realizes that the basic business of the brokerage firm is sales and will operate to keep everyone employed, not to destroy careers!

If You Are Party to an Arbitration

- Always be responsive and courteous; there is no room for attitude, a whining victim persona, major eye rolling, or sarcasm.
- If you need an attorney, usually your firm will provide one.
- If you were found to be at fault, you may need to hire your own counsel.
- You can proceed without an attorney; this is called in pro-per; but you must be prepared.
- When conference calls and meetings are set, be on time.
- Dress professionally but not over the top.
- Don't chew gum.

- Turn your cell phone off.
- Take notes—by Friday afternoon Monday seems like eons ago.
- If using your computer to take notes make sure the panel knows what you are doing
- Tell the whole truth, it's easier to remember, and you are under oath.
- Give the other party whatever is needed in the discovery request. If it is overly broad or burdensome, you have the right to know why certain things are requested or to protest. Don't ignore requests without some sort of agreement or solution.
- Most cases settle long before arbitrating, but if yours proceeds, be professional, calm, and courteous in front of the panel.
- If you have done nothing wrong, the truth will bear out.
- If you would like to become an arbitrator, new applicants are welcome. You can find applications at www.NASDR.com.

Changing Firms, Making Transitions, Signing Bonuses

Moving on is a natural urge. When things appear doomed to failure we want to jump ship. The grass always seems greener on the other side of the street. It is easy to be tempted by the promise of "more," or a situation that is void of your worst problem. Discomfort or annoyance will make you seek a solution. Someone may try to buy you with a juicy signing bonus. Look within first.

Jumping around looks dreadful on your record and causes clients to lose trust. Often you trade one set of issues for another. It is often said that salespeople are the easiest to sell, and I think in our industry this is true. Here are a few points to remember if you are planning to change companies:

- Does the reason you desired to leave have anything to do with something that is a fault of yours? If so, you are just taking your problem to a new firm.
- Is everything being promised in writing? This is especially important if you are accepting a five-year signing bonus/loan.
- Do you have a non-compete clause that prevents you from working for a competitor in a specific geographic area (over and above the requirement to not contact clients)?
- Are you close to a retirement vesting?
- Will you have the same insurance, commute, and other non-tangible benefits?
- Is the company you are moving to on solid ground, not in any type of situation, being bought or sold, or in any other kind of situation that would make your move short-lived?
- Is the company you are moving to in any kind of regulatory firestorm that could harm your reputation by affiliation?

Make sure you are comparing apples with apples. Things you need to examine more closely are: company culture, payout, location, future plans, policies on assistants, connection with the manager (which could change at any moment—managers leave too!), and any promise made "off the books." In other words, if any special arrangements made on your behalf aren't in writing, they could soon become "too bad, so sad" when the manager gets canned for making special deals. Avoid being hung out to dry.

Top producers are frequently recruited for their healthy book of existing business. Make sure yours is portable before moving.

If you decide to accept a signing bonus in the form of a loan (forgiven over a set period of time), know that if you do not see the job through the period agreed to, you will pay back any portion that is due for non-completion of your contract. This is usually an airtight contract and is the reason I advise you to make sure that all you are promised is in writing as well. Therefore, it is wise not to spend it all at once in case it doesn't work out.

Going Independent

Often reps decide that going independent will solve a lot of their issues, and in cases of control you are usually correct. If you have the proper licensing and are capable of running a business it can be a wonderful opportunity to do what you do best the way you want to do it!

There are many logistical issues to work out when opening your own office, all of those will be addressed by the BD partner you select.

There are two things you must consider and be aware of that may not be addressed. One is the fact that a 90 percent payout soon becomes about 40 percent when you are fully staffed and up and running. Many of the things you took for granted will now be your own expense. So do your homework. Research other independents to find the right partner.

Small firms will offer you "start-up money" money in order to compete with the big names you know; be careful. The bonus will fade quickly if your systems don't work efficiently and the operational integrity is lax. No endorsement here, just advice to be thorough in your selection process. Like any marriage, it is a permanent arrangement that is complicated to exit.

Relationships and New Rules for Smaller Accounts

Relationships are the goal of most firms as opposed to one or two transactional sales. It has become apparent that with all the competition out there, the relationship is fleeting and impermanent if it doesn't become a "full service relationship." That means you get all the business there is to have and it is the only way you will hit the million dollar mark. The full service, deep relationships take communication and a top quality service commitment.

Firms are adding financial services such as mortgages, a variety of insurance products, and business loans. Many firms have tried to eliminate the smaller and less profitable client by driving them away from the advisor and to the user-friendly Web site to do their business. The usual benchmark is if the client has twenty five thousand or less, sometimes fifty or less, to send them to the brokerage Web site to do business. So reps are doing this without second thought.

I am here to tell you this is often a huge mistake. Why? A good profiler—someone with the integrity, talent, and concern to learn everything about the client, will often uncover much more! Who is going to give a newly established relationship with a new broker millions of dollars without testing the waters? They didn't get wealthy by investing carelessly!

That being said, after careful interviewing, one might learn the prospect actually does have less than the target amount to invest using a broker, and then it may be appropriate to send them packing. A lot of smaller accounts will impede your performance with service issues. When they do get an inheritance or a rollover, I am sure they will look you up, right? Probably not.

Lose the ego. The funniest line I hear frequently from a fairly new broker who is not fully established is, "I only handle clients with 250K or more." That's a privilege you earn with time, experience, and success. Get over yourself!

Balance—Life and Time for the Kid's Shots

At the center of all careers there is the quest for balance and rightfully so. We work for a reason and work should not be our whole life.

Sometimes people identify so closely with what they *do* rather than who they are that they become off balance and everything becomes more challenging. Sometimes people retire and fall into a state of depression when they are no longer the active lawyer, or practicing physician. Work was their entire reason for being and now it is gone!

Balance is needed with respect to proper rest, exercise, family, and spiritual nourishment, whatever forms those might take. There are four components of "the whole broker," found especially in those who are the most successful. Each represents an equal quarter of the whole and is equally important. Million dollar producers are "whole" brokers.

Become a "whole" broker by tending to each area below:

A. Business Development

(Ample emphasis on Goals, Time Management, Marketing, focus—becoming successful with career)

B. Personal Competency

(Commitment to additional knowledge and both personal and professional development—grow! Read a book a month at least. One a week is better. Be articulate. Take courses. Learn new things. Get additional credentials.)

C. Image

(Dress like pro, be articulate and well read, and sport impeccable manners, and social accoutrements. Be neat and organized; keep your car clean. Ladies, conservative dress and make-up. Gents, please, easy on the cologne!)

D. Personal

(Values, Integrity, Family, Fitness, Faith, and friends)

Establish boundaries and maintain balance in life. Don't sacrifice family, health, and personal time to become successful. The truth is if you are really working smart—making every moment count—you can do this with ease during a regular work day. If you dribble away the day, you will find your self immersed in business late into the evening. "Time-block" your daytime activities to accomplish all you need to complete while at work so you can head home with a clear mind.

So often we need to run an errand or take our child for a vaccination, and it throws our workday into chaos. Companies need to provide a level of comfort for the normal things that give their team a sense of comfort and compassion. Most do. Often the company is open to personal commitments but the advisor is needlessly overly concerned. So set your boundaries and stick to them.

Making your child's doctor appointments a priority will make you a better employee. If you are fully productive the rest of the time, small personal needs are a non-issue.

Fitness and Stress Reduction Methods

It is important to keep your "instrument" tuned, balanced, and healthy. Your body is your vehicle, your computer, and your source of energy. Understand how your body works best! To get to the top and stay there you need to focus on fitness, health, and reduced stress.

Unlike strict regimens that limit this and forbid that, I am a proponent of moderation. Why? The rigid structure is almost impossible to stick to. Small incremental steps will make a world of difference. Besides, the gym is a great place to prospect!

Here are a few basic tips to get you on the path to fitness:

- Exercise, even if it is a daily walk.
- *Get ample sleep.
- If you smoke, quit.
- Always eat a breakfast—it starts your engine.
- Limit alcohol during the week.
- Don't skip lunches.
- Limit coffee to two cups in the morning.
- Try Yoga or meditation to sooth your nerves.
- Limit world news to one or two times a day.
- Replace negative radio news with groovy music.
- Leave work at the office (most of the time).
- Get regular physical checkups.
- Be leery of doctors pushing medications for conditions that can be corrected with the basics mentioned above (they have a quota to prescribe for that Hawaiian trip!).

* What's ample? Some time ago I learned of this experiment to find out how much sleep one needs: For three days in a row, eat a lighter meal and drink no alcohol. Go to bed at the exact same time each night, set no alarm clock. When you awake naturally each day, count how many hours you slept, that's what your body requires every night! Try it, it really works!

Partnerships and Creative Team Development

This is not a brand new trend in the financial services industry, but it has become more popular in the past few years. Advisors form groups of talented advisors who operate as a single sales and service unit, called a team. There are several dynamic business models that have proven successful.

Some of the teams include a very high producing advisor who can no longer manage and service his or her book of business alone. The advisor brings in a "partner," or several partners, and by adding support to his or her efforts the advisor is able to expand and continue to grow the business.

Some teams are not necessarily high producers but rather newer advisors who combine forces and work together to build a business. Often they will diversify their talent by their chosen target market, one advisor taking the retirement tack, and another leaning toward the tax-free marketplace, still another as an insurance specialist or an estate planner. The team will also have administrative support. Clients are handled by everyone on the team as needed.

There are many ways to divide the shared revenue using a variety of criteria. In many cases all the revenue goes into one pot and is shared by a predetermined formula. This is the best way to get everyone totally on board. One of the higher producers might say, "Well that doesn't sound fair." However, if you think about the referral opportunity within the group—meeting prospects you may never had met on your own—it usually works out fine and balances out in the long-run.

Sometimes a successful advisor will promote an assistant to a "junior partner" status, mentor and train them, and replace the assistant with another administrative person who will assist both.

There are many complications that are overlooked in the heat of the planning stage. Attention must be paid to matching individual personalities, clearly laying out all expectations (i.e., who will pay for the licensing fees and operational costs), deciding what to do in the event it doesn't work out, how to solve problems that arise, and having an exit strategy for someone wanting to retire or worse, not fitting in. Everything should be spelled out in writing.

Once the team is formed there should be plenty of communication—at least a weekly meeting to discuss the events of the past week, iron out problems, and share solutions. This can be a weekly breakfast or even dinner to avoid cutting into working hours; but a team will fail without the nourishment of frequent structured and candid communication. Have an agenda and rotate leaders to keep the conversation on track.

Proprietary Products and Services

New brokers have a hard time being humble in this exciting and competitive environment. You want to fit in, you are ordered to make 150 calls a day; but you are unsure of what to offer if a prospect wants to do business with you! To avoid this situation, do two things and do them immediately: learn to profile like no one else can, and learn every product in the marketplace and how it applies. Have I said that already?

Proprietary products are the private label and managed products that can't be transferred out in the event you bolt. Your company offers you an added incentive to "recommend" a certain product or service over others. Sometimes perhaps, they create a disincentive for you to use nonproprietary products by paying less for certain transactions. If the proprietary product meets your approval, of course it is a good idea to work with the firm's in-house products and money managers. It also insures the loyalty of the client! But selecting one product over another should not be purely for monetary reasons. And it should never be a product that is the hot product of the office that day or be mandated to sell by your firm.

The answer is always, and only, this: Do the right thing for the client, determined by the information you gathered and the broad product knowledge you enjoy. Keep good notes, a high level of integrity, and a good dose of common sense.

An NASD arbitration panel would not accept, "Well, that is what we were supposed to sell because—" as an acceptable answer to any a claim of unsuitability. They would accept an intelligent response regarding the performance and the fact that proprietary products are managed close to home and afford ample research and easy access to the money managers—if that is the case.

This takes us back to choosing your firm, and knowing upfront what is and isn't expected of you.

Target Marketing, Affinity Marketing and Shameless Self Promotion

Target marketing is a method of focusing in a specific market you wish to do business with. Who is your ideal client? What group of individuals do you want to sell to and to service? Describe that kind of client and then get busy learning everything you can about the lifestyle of that kind of client.

Affinity marketing is closer to home. Identify a market that you or your family has an affiliation with. It could be church, golf club, or any other organization where you would find warm prospects. This should be a group that you are able to penetrate through alignment with that group's common needs and problems.

Of course, when seeking an area to prospect, everyone chooses doctors and affluent corporate executives, ignoring the lucrative target markets around them. The average doctor today is not wealthy as in days gone by. Extremely wealthy folks are not as plentiful as your average middle American. A well-heeled Baby Boomer probably has more socked away.

If you are in this business as a career change, have you reached out to former contacts at your old firm? The option of prospecting the contacts from a previous career, your friends, and family will at least get you comfortable talking the talk. It is wise to focus on two, no more than three target markets to learn about and become an expert in their needs and challenges.

I once helped a new broker whom I will call Peter. He became an advisor during a career change from being a successful psychologist at a most prestigious university. He left a successful practice to join the world of finance. He felt it was time for a change.

Peter's specialty in counseling was grief and loss. The first target market he chose, and won, was the underserved group of funeral directors in his state. Not only did he do numerous group seminars for them, but they also gave him a constant stream of referrals from their clients' survivors who often had an inheritance but little or no experience in dealing with large amounts of money. How's that for creative?

Peter brought in several million dollars in new accounts in his sixth month as a new advisor!

In some cases advisors "miss the mark" because they are too shy or reserved to approach their affinity groups—the very people who would probably be very supportive, maybe even advocates! The forgotten may have even felt snubbed.

You must practice the art of shameless self-promotion. Let people know what you do and where you work. You will be surprised how many followers from your own network you will have as clients.

Refer back to the beginning of this book; there are many different ideas for finding clients according to your personality and style!

Professional Speaking and Dynamic Seminar Marketing

Why host a seminar and do they really work to generate business? The answer is yes. The concept of prospecting to a number of people at one time is a popular business-building practice. Why present to one or two when you can present to many at the same time?

In today's busy convenience-oriented world, holding powerful and unique seminars can give you an edge in a community as the expert to be seen for financial assistance. Learn every aspect of planning, preparing, and delivering an effective seminar.

Please, don't just produce the usual with your favorite wholesaler as the talking head doing all the work; try creative ways to bring in a crowd and be value added for the attendees. Seminars like these are fun and easy to plan. Try the five unique events below and watch the business roll in.

New to the business and wondering what you have to offer as a new advisor? You might be surprised. The moment you stand in front of a crowd, whether to introduce another speaker or to take the floor yourself, you are the perceived expert. Don't squander the opportunity to make a great and long-lasting impression. It's important to remember that like any other sales call, a seminar requires that you close—ask for the business.

Block the time to do the logistical planning without dedicating your entire week to the event. Consider the following "cheap and easy" seminars that will keep your appointment book full!

Five Cheap and Easy Seminars

With a little planning and some personal savvy, this blueprint will show you the way to hold an effective and profitable event at almost no cost with out any stress.

Let's drill down to the primary reason for hosting a seminar—getting qualified people in front of you, right? Taking that to the next step, what do qualified prospects want?

Prospects don't want all the fluff and fanfare that so many advisors offer at grand and lavish seminars. Most want a genuine benefit, pure and simple. Think about that for a moment. Sometimes they want the interaction with others. Never forget *your* reason for the seminar in the first place-to build your practice!

A Walk Through Seminar History

At one time, seminars were once the hottest items and most lavish events in the financial services industry. In the mid-eighties you could pack a room of hungry prospects to disseminate information over a meal about Limited Partnerships and insurance products like Single Premium Whole Life, the latter which doesn't exist in that structure any more.

Later, all avenues of financial services caught on and prospective clients attended seminars to learn about mutual funds and economic trends from savvy investment professionals seeking to mass market their goods and services.

Throughout the nineties the seminar market was a routine way of reaching new clients and at some point it began to lose its sizzle.

Too much, too many, same old stuff? Who knows? But today, prospects and clients are once again showing interest in the next wave of educational forums. The Baby Boomers are a new breed, hungry to learn and be able to accomplish building a strong financial future. Perhaps it is just a new generation of investors, but more likely is the fact that many very creative ideas have changed the way seminars are delivered.

Savvy Seminars that are Cheap and Easy to Pull Together

First of all, be creative, don't call it a Seminar! Instead hold a *"Shareholders Meeting,"* launch a *"Power Breakfast,"* develop a *"Roundtable Forum,"* form a *"Client Focus Group,"* or a host an *"Old Fashioned 'Tea.'"*

Seminar A. Shareholders' Meeting

Attendees: Usually clients who already have an investment with you and they can bring a friend.

Purpose: Give clients updates and information on the market, often on their particular investments. You might invite all the holders of funds in the Fidelity fund family, for example, and ask a Fidelity spokesperson to give a brief (repeat, *brief*) update. Or you can give the update yourself! Either way, make sure you introduce the program and end the event so that you are the hero of the information exchange.

Script: "Mrs. Jones, we are having an informational meeting for clients invested in the XYZ fund, since you own that fund, I would like to have you join us."

Serve: Simple foods, snacks, coffee in the morning and cold drink in the afternoon. Perhaps a wine tasting with hors d'oeuvres in the evening.

Invitations: Telephone calls, followed by a nicely copied letter type of invitation with details for those agreeing to attend.

Location: Your conference room, local library, church conference room.

Secret: Simplicity—no elaborate and time-consuming planning; no major mailings, very easy to plan and execute. When you hit your target number of attendees, move on to a different date.

Seminar B. Power Breakfast—Free Coffee

Attendees: A guest and usually professionals (sometimes retirees) in the area who would be likely to attend an early morning. Small group of eight to ten.

Speaker: The idea is to invite professionals who are trying to build their practice, like you. You invite a guest professional as a speaker to give a brief presentation and to lead an interactive discussion.

The guest speaker topic should match the target market. For example, a business crowd would appreciate hearing about new laws regarding business; seniors might better appreciate estate-planning information, Boomers might like hearing from a LASIK surgeon or even a plastic surgeon.

Purpose: To give prospects and clients general information about a relevant topic followed by coffee and light refreshments and conversation. To give you a chance to call high net worth professionals seeking new clients and invite them to speak at the event.

Script: "Dr. Kennedy, I am having a morning coffee for several of my better clients and wondered if you would stop by to discuss LASIK Eye Surgery?"

Serve: Simple foods, snacks, coffee, and tea.

Invitations: Telephone calls, followed by a nicely copied letter with details. This is a terrific way to prospect as you seek that professional guest speaker and the attendees!

Location: Your conference room, local library, church conference room.

Secret: Simplicity—no elaborate and time-consuming planning; no major mailings. You can set these kinds of seminars up on a regular basis, monthly—even weekly!

Seminar C. Roundtable Forum

Attendees: Usually clients who already have an investment with you and prospects. This is a good event to hold on a regularly scheduled basis. Book them and then use them as your "reason for the call."

Purpose: very similar to the Power Breakfast but may or may not have a speaker. Without a speaker, a general roundtable discussion is held with the advisor facilitating. Usually some pertinent article or news of the day can be the topic. Cut and copy an item from the morning's *Wall Street Journal* or the U.S.A. Today and make it the focus of the discussion.

Serve: Simple foods, snacks, coffee in the morning and cold drink and half-sandwiches in the afternoon.

Invitations: Telephone calls, followed by a nicely copied letter or a postcard with details. Always ask for an RSVP and a courtesy call to cancel if they cannot make it. If scheduled regularly, hand out a flyer with every encounter or new account opening.

Location: Your conference room, local library, community or church conference room. Small crowd but according to the size of your conference room (probably about ten to twenty).

Secret: Simplicity, held regularly, can be alternated with the Power Breakfast for continuous exposure. No elaborate and time-consuming planning; no major mailings.

Bonus: Get a reputation as the community expert and an excellent communicator!

Seminar D. Client Focus Group

Attendees: Everyone who is qualified to participate in a research project about investment practices.

Purpose: Research. All of your questions answered by the people who matter. Banks and credit unions have done this for years to glean what is important to their clients and members by holding Focus Groups. It is conducted in a very business-like setting with very little free conversation.

Ten good questions should be asked about a specific topic of your choice. Perhaps-what a participant expects and needs from a financial advisor. Maybe-how important online access to an account is. Learn-are people prepared for retirement? Make it relevant to the invited focus group attendees. Caution: be sincere in your efforts to learn the answers to the important questions asked during a Focus Group meeting or host another type of event.

Serve: Coffee in the morning and cold drinks and water in the afternoon; perhaps a tray of cookies. Limit refreshments.

Invitations: Telephone calls, followed by business-like detailed explanation; maybe an advance list of questions to ponder.

Location: Your conference room, local library, community conference room.

Secret: Simplicity; some time-consuming planning; no major mailings.

Bonus1: If the results are unusual you might get the chance to tell the story on a local radio show.

Bonus 2: You have the chance to re-connect when you give the participants the results of your 'survey'.

Seminar E. Host a Tea

A lovely tea! The latest rage!

Attendees: Primarily for women, with or without an existing relationship with you. Brave men are welcome too.

Purpose: To introduce yourself and your services in a unique and lovely fashion; to prospect a group of ten to fifteen guests.

Serve: Simple foods—snacks, elegantly served tea, and a cold drink in the afternoon.

Set the atmosphere of a Tea with accruements such as tablecloths and napkins that can be rented or purchased inexpensively and reused again and again! This can often be funded by a favorite wholesaler. This should feel like a special occasion.

Invitations: Nicely printed, but print more than you need and have the date blank so you can add it for several events. Make sure the invitations use a font you have available on your computer and a standard point size.

Location: Your conference room, hotel, or nice restaurant.

Secret: Some planning required, but plan for a few at the same time, a month apart. Maximize your efforts. Mailed invites followed by a phone call, or call first and send invitation after call. Use a very targeted guest list. Maybe engage the assistance of a vendor to help with the cost.

What a great way to meet a lot of people!

The Power Breakfast and the Roundtable have become popular ways to mass market. These types of seminars afford multiple prospecting opportunities. The idea is to network with CPAs and/or attorneys who need exactly what you need—clients! By inviting them to address your top clients and prospects briefly in a small and intimate roundtable forum where you are striving to bring the latest information and value to your clients, you become the champion. Set dates for the forum—more than one is best. Select your own branding for the name, or call it a "Coffee"— something that sounds casual and enjoyable.

Make sure you are matching the professionals you are partnering with to your target market. Affluent seniors or pre-retirees? Seek estate-planning types. Small business owners, business oriented partners, and so on. Boomers have many interests to consider.

When Planning Seminars You can Call all Day Long!

What a great excuse to make outbound calls. Be sure to prospect your target market with an invitation to learn something that is timely and pertinent—new rules, social security changes, etc. Make it an interesting topic. If you manage to have several dates set, you should be able to host ten or twelve per meeting and fill the spots up quickly.

On a Moment's Notice

Another popular method is the "Pocket Seminar." Have an approved seminar in your hip pocket, ready to go on a moments notice. Make yourself available at the last minute for groups and associations that might have a planned speaker bail out at the last minute. Keep it generic and not self-serving. Your reward will be the opportunity to meet the attendees and be seen as an expert in your field.

Not sure what to present? Right now there are hundreds of interesting and available seminars offered by your product providers. They are pre-planned, usually pre-approved by your firm, and filed with the NASD. The titles are compelling and most have power points and scripts available that can be shortened or lengthened as needed. You can prospect with that! Check them out or develop your own mini-talk and make it dynamic and interesting on a topic of relevance to the economic environment at the time. When creating a topic, specific and numbered benefit titles sell. Try:

- Five ways to______.
- Ten Things You never Knew about_____.
- Three ways to Maximize your______
- Seven things to consider before_____.

Get the idea?

Reaping the Rewards from Seminars!

Whatever forum you choose, make sure you harvest the opportunities that meetings like those will generate using a first-class follow up method. You're the expert and if people came to hear what you have to say, there is a good chance of getting future appointments. Be the consummate professional in dress and in manners. Don't be too modest—tell your guests that you offer these seminars because you are building your practice.

At the close of the event, have an evaluation that, along with the other data-gathering, has two boxes: one that says, "Call me" and one that says, "Do not call me." Mention this form a couple times throughout the meeting and tell attendees to make sure they check one or the other. Tell them if they check "call me," you will call within forty-eight hours. Promise that if they check "do not call me," that you will not call!

Throughout the seminar, when personal questions are asked—questions that won't benefit the whole group—encourage the person to make a note regarding his or her question on the back of the evaluation form, and state that when you call—you will discuss the question then. This will often encourage them to request that call from you!

Final thoughts: Keep it simple and only do a lavish meal if you are courting a group of prospects who don't need that free meal. Make sure your presentation skills are well developed. From the planning to the delivery, always assume the sale! People enjoy learning and will want "more of you," especially if you are competent, confident, and enthusiastic.

Remember to "Script" your Dialogue

Example of a script to use when calling the expert to address the group:

"Mr. CPA, I am a financial advisor here with Value Brokerage, and I am assembling a monthly informational forum for my top clients and prospects. I was hoping to have a CPA (or an attorney, physician, etc) to speak about [insert topic] for about ten minutes, and at the same time have the opportunity to meet new clients. This will be a small informal group. Would you be interested in participating on [date] at [early time]?" (Set up a few dates and times in advance.)

Example of a script to the clients/prospects:

"Mr. Smith, my name is Michael Jones and I am calling you from Value Brokerage to invite you to an interesting and informative breakfast meeting. To add value to my services I am bringing in an attorney (or whom ever your invited) to discuss the newest [insert topic] and how it might impact your financial situation (or other concern). This is a small informal group. Would you be interested in joining us?"

Get in the groove of doing this on a regular basis and it will be come automatic, then sit back and watch the appointments roll in!

Final Thoughts on Seminar Marketing:

- It is a good idea to line up two or three events at the same time, then you can prospect more heavily with this idea.
- The other professionals will come if they need clients, so don't target the guy or gal who is so busy they can't see straight!
- No long speeches, make brief introductions and allow for networking.
- Clients will come if the hook (topic) and invited speaker are interesting and you become the hero!
- Keep refreshments as simple as possible. This project should not be a drain on your time and efforts!
- Often a local library will work out quite well if you don't have a readily available conference room.
- Remember to send handwritten thank-you notes to the other professionals who were willing to help with this project! Send notes to the ones who couldn't make it too—that person might be a future prospect!
- Make sure you have everyone fill out an evaluation! Questions should include: "What did you enjoy? What could we have done better? Will you come to others? Would you like a complimentary consultation from our professional "team" of experts?"
- If you don't think you are a good speaker, then become one! There are numerous and affordable associations that can help you polish up your style and give you confidence. Toastmasters International is one of several. Visit their Web site at: www.toastmastersinternational.com.

- Listen to your voice—tape yourself. Command your platform like a pro. Connect with your audience by looking right into the eyes of the ones in the front rows, they become your 'friends'. Smile when you speak. Prepare in advance—practice what you will say out loud. Remember to breathe.
- Try this exercise to dispel your nerves: Jump up and down and wave your arms, get your body fully engaged. (It's wise to do this out of view of the audience.)

If you're going to go the seminar route, then make sure it results in business and is not merely a busy activity to please your manager. Follow up zealously!

Cold-calling and Warm-calling in Today's Environment

Why is it that 80 percent of the active advisors did not call their clients after 9/11, based on surveys done as late as January 2002?

Cold-calling with all of its difficulties has become somewhat easier because people want to be touched! They are hungry for information and they want to hear from their brokers, but if they are ignored, any broker will do. So therein lies the opportunity where clients long for attention. If you are not calling them, someone else will.

Clients are smart enough to know when the market is rolling on tough times, yet they still want to know that their trusted advisor—the one who promised to be the finest they ever had—is still at the helm. After all, you promised to take care of their money.

Content rich dialog and advance scripting will uncover ways to overcome the paralyzing fears that make you "fold up" from fear of rejection. When you are interesting and comfortable in your own skin, you will find it easy to do the work, deal with rejection, and push on until you reach your goals.

Marketing Like the Pros

You must become obsessive and compulsive about your business. Marketing is the glue that ties your business together. You must become your own shameless self-promoter, a public relations guru, and an accomplished correspondent. On top of all of this you must be competent, capable, and ethical in the business of investment sales.

Communication, courtesy, and compelling marketing materials will help in the attraction stage of your business development and in the retention of many satisfied clients as well. But more important than all of the ancillary tools and tricks of the trade will be your own internal determination and willingness to work harder than you ever intended to: Constantly assessing what works and what doesn't; being willing to reinvent yourself as you go along; giving 200 percent.

Have a backed up data base and efficient gathering system. Keep track of birthdays. Use postcards when it is time to do reviews—stay in touch. Above all, always return phone calls in a timely manner. Block time every day to do outbound work for existing clients.

Gain knowledge of how local papers often welcome articles as fillers, develop a respectable reputation in a small or large community, and find ways to get your name out there!

Learn how to nurture your fans and stay in touch with your advocates. Consider the advantages and disadvantages of newsletter marketing, Web seminars, and scoring opportunities to appear on radio and television as an industry expert. The advantage would be new business, the disadvantage might be busy work that takes you "off your game". Know the differences.

Host a classy client appreciation event just to say thanks for the opportunity to assist you with your financial future. Most importantly, don't allow any of the above activities pull you away from your main responsibility of new accounts and investment sales.

The Power of Branding

"You can't move up if you don't stand out. Regardless of age, regardless of position, regardless of the business we happen to be in, all of us need to understand the importance of branding."

—Tom Peters

As you build your practice it is important to formulate the image you want to convey; this is called branding. It need not be anything elaborate. I am sure the hamburger place that built golden arches had no idea what lay ahead. It can be a catchy name: "Dave Hartman, the man with the Heart," a slogan or a tag line: "We are mobile and will come to you." It could be what you do—the area you specialize in.

There is a story of a rep who asked what the prospect's favorite wine was during the initial meeting. On that prospect's birthday that bottle of wine sent to the prospect. (He became well known for this!) It could be as simple as wearing a certain tie with characters on it or something about your physical characteristics (extremely tall or short); but as you grow and become known, look for markers that will identify you with the community.

Look at some of the interesting commercials today for investment firms. There is branding on integrity and concern; branding on lowest cost in some cases, and branding on "openness and availability," such as the advertisement that the Charles Schwab Corporation uses: "Talk to Chuck."

Regarding your marketing materials, make sure they have a common theme and color. Complete and very professional sets are available at very reasonable costs at www.vistaprints.com and other online providers. Kits include business cards, stationery, folders, postcards—the works!

The Little Things *Do* Count

Maybe you are reading this thinking, "I know all of this." Perhaps the information in this book sounds elementary to you. It *is* basic! Every huge producer I know or know of has the basics down to a science. After all, your goal is to get people in front of you who will become clients through a series of interactions, right? Then consider the "basics"—the building blocks. Without the building blocks in place the whole structure is weakened. Everything else is gravy.

Much like life, the things that create the best outcome are usually the more simple things we do. The most important part of the planning process is to know what you need to do and to make sure you get it done. If anything is a time-waster it needs to go. Time-wasters come in all shapes and sizes and can even masquerade as a legitimate activity. Be mindful of your time. There is only so much of it in each day, and only twenty days or so in each month.

Let's say you have the habit of perusing the *Wall Street Journal* for an hour each day. You need stay informed, right? So that is twenty hours per twenty business days in a month. You spent two and one-half days reading the *Wall Street Journal* during time that you could have been productive.

Over the year that's thirty days per year. I said earlier not to become too analytical, but if you must, *analyze this* and begin today to make every moment count!

Just Like Downtown—Service Like the Ritz

Your clients have a right to know what to expect. Many a complaint stems from a misunderstanding. For example, are your fees clearly explained? How often can clients expect to hear from you, not just about another product or service, but a real discussion to review their portfolio holdings? How involved will your associate or assistant be and has everyone been introduced?

You can avoid quite a few client service problems by picking good clients in the first place and by identifying your service goals in a written mission statement that is given with the first meeting.

It is much harder to land a new account than it is to take good care of one that has already expressed interest in you by opening an account.

This is where time-blocking can really help. Set aside a portion of time every day (the amount will depend on the size of your book) to service accounts. Once that time is assigned, stick to it and don't be reluctant to say you will handle whatever problems that arise during that timeframe. You will have set aside a specific amount of time each day to provide top quality service. Of course, if it is an absolute urgent situation that trumps other blocked activities arises, you must divert; but usually interruptions are routine matters that can be handled later.

What often happens when you intermingle service work with the daily sales activities is that you get sidetracked. Sales and administrative work don't mix very well. So, like the family physician, deal with calls and administrative duties later in the day. If necessary, train people involved in your business to understand that's how you do things.

I know of a successful rep who conveys that on his telephone voicemail recording along with the standard, "Regrettably, trades left on voice mail will not be executed." He has added, ".

. . and all service issues will be dealt with after the market closes."

It often takes an objective observer or a coach to point out the things that really need to change. We all see ourselves differently than others see us. Evaluate the way you work and determine if some changes are in order. However, for positive changes to occur, you must be open and committed to admitting change is needed. So if you find yourself dropping everything to accommodate every request all day long, rethink your methods and try the suggestions above.

Avoiding the Everyday Pitfalls

Although much of this was touched on earlier, it can't be expressed enough. This is my polite way of telling you to keep your nose clean—literally! The frenetic pace that prevails in a brokerage environment can bring a lot of problems along with the benefits.

A newer broker can find himself or herself in the middle of a conflict that will derail progress. He or she may become entangled in the middle of any of a number of environmental and political obstacles.

Environmental and political challenges aren't addressed in any training classes! They include but are not limited to:

- A branch manager with a hidden agenda precipitated by insecurity, prejudices, or ego
- The office gossip—stay clear
- The office cry-baby—pass the tissue box and run!
- The jealous co-worker—be kind
- The boss's spy—be aware and cautious
- Basic office conflicts or misunderstandings—communicate and be humble and open if you are involved or at fault

- Support staff that has an issue with you—same as last point
- Support staff that is incompetent—assist, keep notes, coach-before complaining
- Office romances: Don't do it but if you do, be prepared to handle it! One should move to another firm.
- Know when to shut up! You have two ears for a good reason.
- Drug use: avoid temptation and report if witnessed—it's illegal!
- Corporate etiquette, know the rules and the culture. These include:
    - Eating with finesse, not as though it is your last meal
    - Keep your napkin on your lap and remember to use it
    - Never blow your nose in your food napkin
    - Wash your hands in the restroom
    - If you're invited, you pay
    - Boss or most senior exec always pays
    - Best not to order alcohol even if others do
    - In a classy establishment use softer voice
    - Order something easy to eat
    - Turn you cell phone off during meetings and appointments

Staying on Top and Beyond!

Being successful and maintaining success while growing can be as daunting as getting there in the first place!

Do you remember seeing this earlier? It is in the four steps to a million. If one area is attended to while the other three are neglected, this is a recipe for failure. "Failure" is a word I even hate to use in my vocabulary.

Let's drill down a little more and consider the attributes and traits I have seen in the many million dollar producers (and those on the way) I have had the privilege of meeting.

A. Business Development

You give ample emphasis on goals, time management, marketing, and focus:

This means that you continue to learn and grow in your knowledge and in your practice. You use tools to stay focused and leave nothing to chance. You are a heat-seeking laser looking for your target, which is a goal that is written out in a one-page plan and viewed regularly. You know what you will be doing every hour of the day and every day of the week because you make appointments for your activities with Time-blocking. Time really is money and that is perfectly clear to you now.

You have a marketing plan in place but if the result of the plan is not what you hoped it would be, you replace it with something else. You will avoid the office gossip, the negative whiner, and mind your own business. You will leave your ego at the door.

B. Personal Competency

You are competent! You have made a commitment to growth, excellence, and personal and professional advancement:

You have made a total commitment to additional knowledge and professional development—to grow! Read a book a month at least, fiction or non-fiction. It stimulates thinking. Embrace stimulating hobbies and challenges.

You make sure you have thorough and complete knowledge of all of the tools and products available to you. You join organizations to help in your thrust for improvement, like Toastmasters for seminar speaking. You set goals to acquire additional designations, but never at the expense of your business development. You study business periodicals—it stimulates the creativity. You read them on your own time! You take courses offered by your firm. You learn to garden or find other ways to reduce stress. You are always striving for a higher level. People often describe you as "positive, energetic and smart".

C. Image

You dress like pro, you are articulate and well read, and sport impeccable manners and social aptitude:

You dress for success. You always strive to be the best dressed in your office. You ignore "casual day" and dress like a winner. You make sure your elocution is clear and distinct. You lose grammatical slang. Your glasses are clean. You smile warmly but sincerely or not at all. You are friendly to support staff—always. You are courteous and kind to everyone. You never judge anyone by their appearance.

D. Personal

This includes values, integrity, family, faith, and friends:

You give equal energy and commitment to your family, whether you have a brood of ten or a golden retriever to greet you at the end of the day. Your home life is important, whatever that means to you. It is a safe place to kick off your shoes and relax—a place where you are loved and comfortable. Integrity is so important to you and you always take the high road. Because you do, you will be assured a good night's sleep forever. If time permits, you volunteer. You do charitable work at a local food kitchen at holiday time (this can be a real eye-opener, helping your perspective). You take care of the inner you as well as the outer you. You select friends carefully and you remember that to have friends means you have to be a friend as well.

If you are able to incorporate the above characteristics, habits and attributes into you life, along with the best practices spelled out in this book, you are definitely on your way to the top!

Leadership

Branch and Regional Managers, Team Leaders and Reps with Assistants: The most important thing you can do is to provide true leadership

Are Leaders Born or Made?

Leaders differ from one another in countless ways. But they share common features: profound passion and a desire to succeed. Leaders own their passion and make no apologies or excuses for their deep-rooted convictions. They are fervent about their missions, and their missions drive them. They are often considered "different."

Can this passion be developed or do leaders emerge from the tender protection of their mother's womb with a destiny to lead ingrained in their DNA?

I believe leaders are born *and* made. While the necessary ingredients to lead may already be deep inside of each of us, these innate leadership skills can be unleashed with the proper care. If you are managing a team of investment reps and can get them behind your goals, the sky is the limit. Leadership can make that happen.

Leaders Close to Home

Who do you know in your world who demonstrates strong leadership? Is it a boss, a friend, or a family member? Who seems to enjoy a pied piper-like charisma that moves others to action effortlessly and positively?

Imagine having the ability to manage a sales team with unlimited enthusiasm and a commitment to your stated goal. Think about the problems that could be resolved when your reps pull together behind you as a respected and powerful leader. It is possible, and this section will share some proven methods of developing leadership and management skills that will result in added revenue, loyal followers, and other promotions.

The Fallacy of Leadership Training

Corporate boardrooms are abuzz with the benefits of leadership training. But leadership training alone does not create effective leaders. Only when you combine it with sales management skill development will you likely achieve the results you seek—employee retention, job satisfaction, loyalty, and increased productivity.

Leadership, after all, is the frosting on the cake of competent managing skills. Don't believe it? Ask yourself the following question: can a successful, organized, and competent manager survive without leadership attributes? Most definitely. Can a dynamic and charismatic leader prevail in a corporate setting without management skills? Usually not.

Managers vs. Leaders

To grasp the difference between a manager and a leader, and to determine where you or your team leaders fit on the "leadership scale," ask yourself following questions:

- When you walk into a room of your direct reports, do they suddenly become quiet or do they enthusiastically invite you to join in the conversation? *(If invited in you are more of a leader than a boss!)*
- When you have a tough goal or deadline, do your team members get behind you and make it happen or do you sense that they secretly hope you fail? *(A competent*

leader will always have the full support of his or her staff!)

- Do you manage based on your own style or do you make it a point to really understand your people before deciding on a management strategy? *(A leader cares and is sensitive to the needs of his or her people.)*
- Are you tough but fair? Structured, but flexible? *(Strong leadership means more than being a "nice person.")*
- Do you go by the book but freely explain the consequences of not doing so? *(Rules are important, communication is equally so.)*
- Do you understand that your responsibility to manage or lead a team does not include the luxury of liking or disliking anyone—that you must treat everyone the same regardless? *(Without absolute fairness you can't even consider yourself a leader.)*

Promoted from the Ranks—Developing Management Skills

A common mistake is feeling that your service as a top producer promoted to management is enough to be a fine manger and leader. You will at least have the gift of knowing how it feels to be in the shoes of your direct reports, but there is most likely a lot to learn, unless you have a strong background in management.

Being a competent manager paves the way to become a powerful leader. Competence begins with knowing what needs to be accomplished and not playing favorites. This is hard in a sales team where you usually have a vested interest in the outcome. Most managers are overly concerned with being liked. This desire inevitably impedes their ability to lead and manage effectively.

Likeability is often confused with leadership qualities. But you will never please everyone all of the time. Pandering to this natural insecurity will make you appear weak and malleable—

period. Accept that and move on. (You are entitled to respect, however, but that is earned rather than demanded.)

The first step in developing management skills is to ensure that your actions are governed by integrity. The commitment to integrity ensures a comfort level that allows flexibility. Why? If you avoid the slightest perception of impropriety, your reputation as one who takes the high road will precede you. Cut corners and bend too many rules, be inconsistent in your values, and you will be on the company radar screen as a loose cannon—someone to be watched, or worse, fazed out. You have seen it happen, I am sure.

Becoming a Top-Notch Sales Manager on the Road to Successful Leadership

Managing is not about power, but effectiveness. A successful sales manager keeps his or her ego in tow and learns everything necessary to understand the rules governing human resources. This includes regulations issued by the state and city and most importantly by the firm. The firm may interpret state and federal rules differently—either more strictly or more leniently—because companies often prefer to add their own spin. The firms own internal policies will always trump state and federal regulation.

New sales and branch managers: if you have been promoted through the ranks, you may seek mentoring to learn what you need to comprehend as a manager. Here are other techniques to consider for developing your skills and becoming a top-notch manager:

- Research company policy by reading the employee handbook. This is an often overlooked tactic of becoming a better sales manager. Flag areas you may need to refer to (in sales, it may be handling unmet production quotas).

- Learn about the senior team and what is most important to each team member and to the team as a group. Companies, like families, have different cultures and goals. Make sure they know you, too. Be warm and outgoing when meeting in the halls or elevators. Have a recent success on the tip of your tongue.
- Learn how to recruit talent and how to interview appropriately. Remember, you are interviewing folks who know how to "sell"! Improper interviewing and the selection process seem to be an ever-expanding source of lawsuits. If protection of your firm is top on your list, you will be highly valued by your superiors.
- Make sure you dress the part, that your hair and grooming is consistent with what is acceptable in your firm. Your manners should reflect good breeding. (A major recording studio might have different expectations than a private bank. Know the score!)
- Be on time yourself as good example. Use time management techniques effectively and keep an organized work area. Maintain accurate records and files.
- Communicate like a pro. Use handwritten thank-you notes frequently whenever the opportunity arises. Be sensitive to the support staff and every other person you encounter. Use e-mail and communication software to the maximum extent possible, especially if your firm has made a significant investment in technology. Block time each day to reach out through various methods, including phone, fax, and voicemail messages.
- Learn something new every day and read a business or sales efficiency book a month, minimum. Don't stagnate. Grow, blossom, and move through your career with increasing finesse and confidence.

- Journal, and encourage your direct reports to do the same. At the end of the day, spend ten minutes wrapping up thoughts and ideas that were sidelined during the day.

When times are tough, be mindful of the timeless advice I once received from my mentor and boss for many years, the president and leader of a $30 billion bank investment program. To resolve a situation that was more gray than black and white, she reminded me to take the high road: "Light always shines in the darkness." In my darker moments that comment was my strength.

Attending Leadership University-Within

Once you establish competency as a manger, it is time to work on your leadership skills. Remember, everything you need is within you.

The first thing to do is to examine how you view your people. It's important to know who your people are and what's important to them. Satisfied employees will provide the wind for your "sales."

This is where the "God gave you two ears and one mouth" adage is critical—be a good listener. Fight the urge to interrupt and make early comments.

Fairness isn't always easy to accomplish—as humans we often tend to have some people we like more than others. Departing from the luxury of selection based on personal taste is the earmark of a great leader.

Learn Who They Are, and What's Important to Them

If I asked you today about your top people, how much could you tell me? Pick your most valued employees and try to answer the following questions about them:

- What is important to them? Do they have kids to pick up after school? Are they concerned with their job performance?
- Where did they work before coming to your firm? Where do they live? How long is their commute every day?
- Are they caring for a sick parent? Do they have a handicapped child?
- Are they happy, sad, or indifferent?
- What do they do in their leisure time?
- Do they rent or own their own home?
- Are their children good students?
- Are they trying to have children and can't?
- What do they look like and could you describe them accurately?
- What kind of cars do they drive?
- What music do they like?
- What is their favorite sport?
- When is their birthday?

Now run through the same exercise using your least favorites. Did you know the answers? The first step in effective leadership is to know who your people are and what motivates them. The second step is to effectively utilize the information you glean for everyone's benefit—no favorites!

Many questions cannot be legally asked, such as marital status, sexual orientation, and age, as well as other issues. However, when learned through the course of a normal conversation, it is acceptable, as long as you don't use any information to discriminate in any way.

For instance, suppose someone confided in you that she was trying desperately to become pregnant. If that confidential information influenced your decision to promote her or led to a negative consequence for her, you would likely be in violation of federal law, putting both you and your firm at serious risk.

Special Meetings: Building a Team That Considers You the Leader

The following exercise is one of the most enjoyable aspects of developing leadership because it gives you instant rewards and sets the course for your new goals:

Plan a meeting for a day when everyone who works for you can attend. Have an extra nice lunch brought in and do a few extra things to make it special. I often lay out crayons and colored pencils, candy kisses and tablets. The message is that this is not a meeting to convey negative news or anything remotely uncomfortable.

Open the meeting by announcing your plan to become a better manager, to learn more about them, and to build a stronger team. Declare your desire to accept all input, positive as well as negative. Plan a couple of teambuilding exercises that will foster relationships among team members.

Try pairing them off, having one interview the other, followed by the interviewer presenting what they learned about the other to the entire group. Select three things in advance they should learn about the person being interviewed, such as favorite movie, secret passion, and most admired person and why. After the first group is finished, switch.

When everyone has been interviewed, have each person stand and give a three-minute talk on the coworker just interviewed. The idea is to get them talking to one another.

Another good warm-up exercise is to ask everyone to bring their own baby picture, post them all on a board, and have a

"Guess Who This Is" activity. That is always a fun team-builder.

The crayons and pencils allow them to doodle creatively. It's entertaining!

The Essential Moment of Truth—It's your Turn Now

In order to improve as a leader, it's essential to solicit feedback from your reports. This requires bravery and nerves of steel. At some point in your team meeting, pull a flip chart to the center of the room and select a person in charge for this exercise. Announce that you are going to leave the room for forty-five minutes so they can talk about *you.*

Ask the group to write a list of things on the flip chart that you could do better. Tell them this is their chance to vent and speak honestly. Encourage them not to seek approval by writing complimentary things. Also, it's important to remind them not to list things that are out of your control, but to focus on things that you can modify.

After about forty-five minutes, return to the meeting. Spend time going over the results after you rejoin the group. Resist the urge to be defensive. There will be something that stirs emotion in you—guaranteed. It is such a natural reaction, especially if something you do has been misunderstood. You will have plenty of time to work this out later.

At the end of the meeting, open your appointment book and book one-on-one meetings with every direct report. Make it a lunch if possible. At lunch, plan to complete the get-to-know-you exercise in private and raise a couple of points brought up when you were out of the room.

By the way, regardless of your company policy, where lunches among employees are often not applicable to an expense account, never allow a direct report to pay for his or her own lunch. If you are too cheap to pick it up yourself bring it from home or make it a coffee date instead!

When making one-on-one field or office visits, use a notebook to record everything you can about this person after the meeting, from birth dates, to favorite sports or music, goals, needs, and requests made of you. Convey and discuss what you learned from the meeting. Ask how they prefer to be managed. Have a page for each employee and keep it updated. Your employees will be amazed that you are keeping track of things and showing a personal interest.

This notebook need not be kept a secret if it makes you uncomfortable to do so, and should never contain anything illegal or private. It is a journal for you to remember the important things in a conversation, and to guarantee follow-up. I always preferred to keep my notes private; it is your choice. After each meeting I would spend a little time in the car memorializing what I learned.

When you know your direct reports well enough to answer the questions listed earlier, you are truly on your way to becoming a leader. When they know you really care about their issues and concerns, the sky is the limit!

The Carrot Always Works Better than the Stick!

Most problems can be solved without drastic punitive measures. Sometimes a heavy hand is needed, especially with compliance issues where there is a requirement to record how violations are dealt with. But most often, problems can be solved with communication, training, coaching, and a sincere effort to find a solution. Using the leadership model, a similar problem might be resolved differently depending on the rep in question.

Help Where *They* Need Help

I am sure you never thought I was going to get to the heart of the business—selling! This is where some managers take the wrong path to mentoring a rep. Neither good nor bad, right nor wrong, managers will attempt to assist a floundering rep by suggesting ideas that worked so well for themselves! The manager was a top producer and this worked for him or her, so it should work for everyone!

This is where it is important to know your rep, know what drives him or her and what keeps the rep up at night. This is also the part where knowing *all* of your reps as outlined above helps you cross-pollinate and share good ideas because as managers we don't have them all!

I have seen blanket mandates for one marketing idea or another fail because everyone is different! Later, when a rep I knew failed and was released after using the mandated method, she went on to be a superstar in another firm using a method that better fit her personality!

Newbies Often Need *Different* Guidance

As a rookie, or a seasoned pro needing a fresh start, reps confront a host of challenges, not the least of which are their own personal, and often obscure, stumbling blocks. Recognizing these obstacles early will help you to provide appropriate counsel. Here's a list of the five most common personal pitfalls reps encounter, and the best strategies for overcoming them:

On the road to building or rebuilding their business, ask new reps to consider these common rookie challenges—and the strategies that will help them to overcome them. Cut this out and share it in a morning meeting for rookies. Make the meeting interactive.

You think you're too young. Many advisors with no prior business experience fear that age will be an impediment to landing accounts with older, wiser prospects. If you're a rookie, you might feel that your twenty-three-year-old face is like a neon sign flashing "inexperienced!" for the world to see. You might fear that your youth will prevent people from trusting you or believing what you have to say, resulting in lost opportunity. And if you're winging it or unprepared, your fear might very well be valid.

Solution: Take heart—as a recent graduate, you're more likely to be on top of the newest ideas, technology, and insights. Focus on showcasing your professionalism, preparation, product and service knowledge, and communication skills. Stress the strengths of your firms experience and service. If you commit to becoming the best that you can be, you'll ensure that you present not only a professional image, but also a memorable and impressive one. And ultimately, your age can become an asset—you'll notice your clients remarking, "He [or she] is so sharp, particularly for such a young person."

Fear of failure. This presents an overwhelming challenge for rookie advisors. On top of your own personal goals and desires, you're dealing with your boss who is probably monitoring your activities and productivity on a weekly basis—as well as the basic stress of earning a living. Fear of failure is a very real concern in a business where you're tackling a range of duties, but where your main responsibility is seeing people who have a need for investment products and services, and being the provider of that service.

Solution: Never waste a moment. Make every minute count. Be organized. Listen to positive messages and tapes and relax with uplifting entertainment. Stay physically active, balanced, and rested. Plan and measure your progress. Review your plan and regroup when necessary. Stay away from the office whiner and spend as much time as possible in the company of successful colleagues. Listen to world news once or twice per day, but not constantly. If you are doing all of this, there will be no room for fear and worry and the downward cycle these feelings perpetuate. Activity results in success.

Kicking back too soon. "Success fever" can strike suddenly if you've had an awesome month of business. The symptoms? You spend a lot more time out of the office and on the golf course or at long lunches celebrating your prowess and early success. In some cases it's a daily trip to Nordstrom's. Then you have a month of zeros and can't figure out what went wrong.

Solution: Celebrate success by doubling whatever you did to contract the fever in the first place—setting new goals and adding creative activities to expand your business. Go for the burn!

Lack of confidence. This malady strikes at everyone's heart. Barbra Streisand has candidly admitted to suffering stage fright, famous athletes often question their phenomenal success on national television, and even presidents have expressed doubts about their ability to lead the nation. Knowing that you're not alone is comforting, but how do you climb out of that awful black hole?

Solution: First, make sure you that work diligently toward becoming a consummate professional and that your lack of confidence doesn't stem from inadequacies that can be solved through knowledge and research (i.e., know every product and service your firm offers, and how to present it). For those normal fears, keep a success journal. Every time you accomplish a goal, write it down. Keep a file of notes and cards you receive from satisfied clients and well-wishers. Label it your "smile File" Never utter a self-deprecating comment. Program yourself to avoid those who are negative and review your good qualities regularly. As you think, you are. Remember, knowledge is power. Power is confidence. Confidence is compelling.

Inadequate work ethic. Beware of this trap. You might have picked up some bad habits at school or during summers when work was "just a job." Maybe you never had to perform according to the level of expectations you're laboring under now. This may not be your fault but you still need to change your habits. If you are chronically late, sloppy, poorly dressed, or insensitive to corporate culture and values, you will be among the many who "wash out" of the business.

Solution: Take a personal and professional inventory. Make sure you are well informed and competent by learning, participating, and engaging in research. Watch those who are experienced and respected, and emulate them. Dress well. Avoid gossip and company bashing—leave that for the folks who are on the train to nowhere. Always give 100 percent of your effort and take full responsibility for your actions. Keep the best interests of your clients uppermost in your mind. Avoid office romances and other shenanigans. Look sharp, speak well, and be a team player. Once you've cleared these hurdles you'll be on your way to reaching your highest potential and joining the ranks of the successful, happy, wealthy, and well-adjusted top-performing advisors.

"Work for two years like no one else will and you will live the rest of your life like no one else can!" Anonymous.

Best practices for Sales Managers: Here are some ideas to improve sales skills and other best practices:

- Discuss time management
- Ensure product knowledge is there
- Give public recognition for success
- Publicize production frequently
- Encourage team-building
- Assign mentors to new reps
- Encourage community work
- Catch them doing something good!

Remind Sales Reps: You have *one responsibility*—find people who need help with their financial future and make appropriate recommendations. Everything else is secondary—important, but secondary. If you can't sell, if you don't "close," if you don't uncover prospects, you are doomed to a different career. If you are doing this chances are your road will be pretty smooth and your ,manager will value your contribution.

Mentoring

So often managers act as though they are in competition with their reps, especially if they were promoted from the ranks. You should be helping them grow professionally because the better they become, the better you look!

Arrange wholesaler guidance—they often have the pulse of the industry and know unique sales ideas. Coach the wholesalers and direct them to be supportive and specific in areas your folks need help. You might be surprised at how helpful they can be.

Teamwork

Have a project of the month where everyone will work together as time allows on one project. It might be creating a job description for an assistant or developing a seminar. It could be a brainstorming session about sales presentations. Challenge them to come up with a solution for a troublesome problem. Get them working together as a unit.

Communication

Keep everyone informed. Time-block communication activities to ensure they happen. Use a variety of methods to reach out and to keep life interesting. Send faxes, e-mails, phone broadcasts, messages and arrange frequent but brief conference calls. Of course, the most impactful approach is personal contact. Use personal notes, and newsy letters. Install an office chart to post production on a daily basis. Plan a sales meeting in January for every month of the year and make it an event that is productive and worthwhile. Make sure everyone enters it on their calendar. Have a special lunch brought in. Find reasons to give awards. Don't fill up the time with a bunch of talking heads, but instead, let the reps help plan it and make it dynamic. That's how you build a team!

Measure and Monitor

You know this is important. Make sure you keep tabs on all production, trends, and changes. Publish both good news and unpleasant news.

Many managers send reports out only when numbers are off and that's not leadership. Statistics need to be seen more often than once a month too.

Think Strategically

If you don't have a plan, why should they? Build a blueprint and share it with your team; keep in mind that the best plan is brief and visible. Pass it around and ask for comments and suggestions to be noted on *your* plan document. Spend thirty minutes a day reviewing your plan and the results to date. Plan for the next level as accomplishment occur.

Creativity

Welcome all ideas and implement the best ones. More heads are much better than one. People will bring you ideas that worked in other firms. Teams are stronger than singular efforts. Dedicate a part of every meeting to idea generation only. Reward the best ideas. Leave the judge out of brainstorming meetings.

Occasionally-Evaluate Your Own Progress

Are you exhibiting leadership traits?

- Active Listening
- Genuine concern for your team

- Advocacy for their needs
- Support across the board
- Encouragement and kindness
- Provide coaching
- Empowering them to manage themselves
- Generous when possible
- Cautious judgment
- Avoid comparisons
- Make sure reps have time for family

Use Your Gifts—Intuition is a gift

Emotional Intelligence (EI) starts with recognizing how emotions affect our actions. Daniel Goleman, one of the leading researchers in the field of emotional intelligence, asserts that the rational mind takes a moment or two longer to register and respond than the emotional mind. The first impulse, he claims, is in the heart, not the head.

If Goleman is correct, then shouldn't our intuition serve us well in all situations? It's there to guide us and we all have experienced this. As managers seeking solutions, often logic will override intuition in an important decision. Later, reflecting on the outcome, the discarded instinctive response may have afforded a better solution. I am certain if you ponder this, it has probably happened for you too.

Recognizing your inner leader

We all have intuition, feelings, and perceptions. Successful people often engaged this gift without realizing it existed.

Leadership requires a total activation of our hearts. As I said before, leadership is the frosting on the cake of competency. Leadership from the heart makes life easier and more enjoyable. Your team will support you, walk on hot coals for you, and cover your back. If you are a dynamic leader, you will find immense pleasure in you work, higher value in people, and less stress in your life.

Heart-centered leadership involves tuning into feelings that may be buried or considered too feminine, or too "touchy feely". Men are taught to be tough and women are taught to be gentle. That's a fact. Although the Baby Boomer generation is a more sensitive lot, there is still a lot of machismo in the male corporate world.

Leadership, like managerial competency, demands fairness in all things. To achieve fairness, a leader must have an open mind and be a good listener. A leader is able to care, and routinely practices the Golden Rule. A leader gives credit to the team and reciprocates with communication, recognition, and advancement.

Make it a point to read up on emotional intelligence. Dig deep within yourself and objectively study who you are. List your strengths and weaknesses. Ask friends and colleagues to describe them also. Do their assessments of you resemble your self-assessments?

Remember to trust your intuition; it is the greatest gift and is there to guide you.

A Final Word on Navigating Human Resources

It is interesting how many "human resource" (HR) departments deal with the duties of their world as though there wasn't a human being in sight.

HR becomes a labyrinth of rules and regulations, interpretations of the law, and administration of the company policies and procedures, forgetting for whom the policies were created—the people.

Human resource departments are usually involved in every aspect of your day-to-day activities as a manager. From hiring practices to the company picnic and from the first advertisement for an advisor to the termination of a top sales rep who has been the subject of praise for the past several years, HR was involved.

Yes, you need to be certain that you follow personnel policies in place and to comply with all state and federal regulations. You also need to make sure that your managers, reps and other direct reports have the knowledge and the skills needed to act on your behalf and in the best interest of the employee and the firm, thereby avoiding awkward and litigious situations.

Be aware that your human resource department, if familiar with the investment business, is concerned with the following:

- Are employment contracts and registered rep agreements thorough and consistent?
- Is there an employee manual and/or a compliance manual and is it required reading for all new employees?
- Is your compensation plan and commission grid profitable for you and for the retention of quality reps?
- Are job descriptions clear and specific?
- Are consequences for not meeting production requirements spelled out and enforced fairly and professionally and are they in writing?
- Is training offered where needed?
- Are performance reviews done regularly and uniformly?
- Are retirement plans and benefits available?
- Is there a written vacation policy?

One might wonder with all of this detail regarding administration, how can leadership be engaged? By aligning yourself with your firm's HR department and educating your people on why it is important, you gain legitimacy and credibility. Both are essential for strong leadership.

Avoid miscommunication! Often HR departments aren't fully aware of the fine distinction investment programs enjoy and may need guidance with regards to sales, quotas, and how commissioned reps are handled with regards to time off. A rep may often work weekends and evenings, in addition to the regular work week. It is usually more of an exempt position, rarely by the time clock routine.

I once worked on a project where everything discussed regarding HR was offered with a wink or a rolling of the eyes. The manager referred to HR as "they." This only made the manager look small and the employees disrespectful as well as confused.

Embrace your company culture and convey that to your team. They will fall in step and emulate your own positive attitude.

As for using your emotional intelligence when hiring and recruiting, how can you not have a feeling one way or another about a candidate? Simply incorporate those feelings into your decision-making without overlooking the proper HR processes. It is possible to use all of your talent when selecting a candidate.

A good leadership tactic when hiring is to make sure the person being considered will fit in with the rest of the group by bringing the team into the interview process. Have a couple your top people do a second interview. This will serve two purposes: it will make them feel important and capable of assisting you as well as help you to identify a worthy candidate.

Dealing in the intuitive world can create problems with the black-and-white world of HR, and vise versa. There is not a lot of room to negotiate in this area, but there is always a place for instinct used correctly and wisely.

Making the Most of Recognition and Rewards

The best motivator is recognition. Finding people doing something well and making a big deal about it is the cheapest and fastest way to improve performance.

Some firms send out a sales report at the end of every month. On report day everyone is either jubilant or embarrassed, but the next day it's all over. If possible report results frequently! Daily is best!

Write positive notes to the people leading the pack and never publicly criticize those at the bottom. Those who see their name at the bottom are reminded that they have work to do. Send voicemail broadcasts out to announce the top five and to further publicize the results. This is a proven way to immediately increased business.

Privately, I would write an encouraging note on a report to those struggling saying, "I know you are having a awful month; let me know if I can help out," or, "This is better than last month, keep it going!"

> Make sure you speak the language. I often referred to this aforementioned attitude of compliance as "carrying the company banner." A new employee called me about three days after an orientation meeting and said that she had looked high and low but was unable to locate this company banner; could I direct her to one? Although we both had a good laugh, it was a reminder to make sure we are all speaking the same language.

My office manager used happy face stickers and all sorts of little elementary stamps to make comments in individual notes. He would send an "Attaboy" note along with a small bag of M&Ms (representing "Money in Motion"). What always amazed me is that these six-figure employees loved it. On a super busy week or during travel, if we neglected to send notes out we would get calls asking if we forgot. Each and every one of us has a child inside, and it can be personally rewarding to let the kid out to play.

When our senior management team realized how effective these little rewards and recognitions were, we initiated awards for team spirit and best mentor, most improved or most flexible. I consistently gave them more and more to strive for and more opportunities for the old pat on the back.

Whatever business you are in, find ways to track as many aspects of good behavior that you can. Publish it consistently and across every department. Keep your people in the limelight as often as you can. If there is a company newsletter, make sure your department gets a little space for news and updates. Other departments will begin to learn what it is that your department does, and during unfortunate but necessary corporate realignments, your people will have a good chance at being relocated within the firm.

Cliff Notes: Leadership Best Practices:

1. Encourage team members to bring problems to you, along with solutions.
2. Allow them to make decisions and think processes through independently.
3. Know your people and figure out the best way to make them more productive.
4. Create simple recognition awards and present them in a group setting.

5. Communicate by multiple methods frequently (i.e., phone, e-mail, and broadcast messages).
6. Hold regular purposeful meetings and have them participate in the planning.
7. Remember birthdays and anniversaries as much as possible.
8. When a problem arises, make no judgment until all the facts are studied.
9. Stop fixing—let people be responsible for the job they were hired to do.
10. Remember common courtesies such as, "Hello," "Thanks," and "Can I help you?"
11. Handle serious problems quickly or delegate them a more suitable department.
12. Know the company policies. Understand and follow HR policies.
13. Read at least one personal growth book every month.
14. Keep your own life balanced and stress free and encourage employees to do the same.

Include Stress Reduction in Your Leadership Strategy

Experts say stress can occur in both positive and negative situations. Believe it or not, there are stories of lottery winners having heart attacks after learning they won millions.

As an effective leader, you can reduce the day-to-day stress for your team members in the following ways:

- Instill confidence through training and coaching.
- Recognize the smallest accomplishments with praise and positive feedback.
- Encourage life balance and reaffirming belief in the need to have a life outside of work.
- Champion physical activity by finding deals to local gyms or providing in-house fitness facilities if the budget allows.

- Never ever discuss one employee with another. It will get out.
- Help employees manage their time by teaching them to use time-blocking methods and other time management techniques.
- Make time for everyone, and show no favoritism.
- Make eating lunch mandatory.
- Bring in an expert to discuss "desk yoga" or other relaxation techniques.
- Let them know you aren't perfect and that you care about their success.
- Think it through carefully before you deliver bad news of any kind.

What drives you? What gets you up and out in the morning? It might be spiritual. It may be worldly, or love for your family and children. It might be a combination. Be in touch with yourself enough to know who you are and what you stand for.

Work

Keeping in mind that we are striving for leadership qualities, your choice of work must be of the highest order. Seek an opportunity that lifts you and allows you to do good deeds and be respected.

Any job or position that feels "wrong" will not fulfill you, but will impede your progress towards being a leader.

Don't make the common mistake of over-identifying with your position at work. Are you a branch manager, an executive VP, an attorney, or a husband and father? Are you a vice president of marketing, a registered rep, or mom and wife? Keep your priorities straight.

Leading by example

If you consider yourself a leader, then your natural expectation is that people will follow you. Your people will look to you and your own behavior as a guideline to follow.

They will look up to you, support you, and look for direction.

That's the good news. The bad news is that they will copy your style whether your behavior is good or bad. After all, if you take two-hour lunches, why shouldn't they? You can say because you are the boss and you said so; but that is about as far way from leadership as you can get. The solution is to set an example of what you expect and it will be followed without question.

On a recent project in a financial institution I was only the project manager/consultant, but it drove me nuts that most people drifted in between nine-thirty and ten in the morning. I never commented on this because it really wasn't my place to do so. However, I started arriving at or before seven-thirty, which is easy to do on location, away from home, and other responsibilities.

By the conclusion of the project most of the people in the office were coming in much earlier, saying how pleasant it was to work before the phones began ringing. Remember this illustration as a simple reminder about leading by example.

A Final Word on Integrity

In perfectly ethical situations you might be asked to put your ethics on hold momentarily. Don't do it. If a manager or your boss made the request, report the indiscretion to human resources immediately. Why? The minute you don't play, you are blacklisted. Reporting the infraction will protect you once recorded. Also, keep accurate notes of the situation.

Consider Enron and their infamous accounting firm. Or Martha's situation. Those could have ended before they began with more ethical people willing to speak up.

Not snitching may be a sign of being "cool" in fifth grade, but in corporate America your first loyalty should be to the company that signs your checks and puts food on your family's table.

Wrong choices would include anything that is immoral, illegal, or even remotely connected to activities that are. Perception is reality. You know what they are.

If a leader has established integrity and always takes the high road he may be out of a job. As difficult as it might be to find another job, it would be far easier than breaking the law and having something come back to haunt you years later.

Putting It All Together

You obviously desire to become a leader or you wouldn't be reading this section of the book.

I hope you realize by now that although some leaders may be born to lead, others are developed along life's path.

Only you can reinvent yourself to inspire and motivate million dollar producers. When you do so you will reap the benefits as well. It is within you to command respect and admiration rather than fear and disdain. You can become a respected leader—one who shepherds his or her employees to their highest potential. And while most of what you need is within, the actual process requires you to look outside and to learn about each and every person who relies on you as their sales manager.

It isn't about you alone; it is about the group as a whole. Your management style must become chameleon-like—ever-changing. Rather than expecting everyone to conform to your wishes and demands, no matter how worthy, try instead to adapt to the personalities and style of the people you are managing.

For All of Those on the Path To a Million

Keep in mind that it doesn't matter if you are new, connected, or from a rich family. These are clearly advantages, but a lack of them is not a deal-killer or a career-breaker.

People buy people. Every investment firm has the same products to offer. Sales are often more art than science. It is a continuous learning process, where listening is often more important than speaking, and learning should be your food for success. People will want you as much as the things you recommend.

Food for Thought

Change your mindset! Contemplate each bullet point for an entire day until it plays in your memory by itself:

- Excellence is product knowledge, people skills, enthusiasm, integrity, and balance.
- Remember the value of your time, effectively managing it is critical to get to the million dollar level. Leave nothing to chance.
- "Work for two years like no one else will and you will live the rest of your life like no one else can." (I wish I knew who said that!)
- Know that there are people out there who will open an account with you, you just have to find them. You have to offer a benefit to them, they will spot self-centered intentions or "bull-oney."

- Work out a personal commercial about who you are and what you do. Make it rich with available benefits to the client, not ego.
- Work from carefully crafted scripts that are your words written in advance and that will put you two or three years ahead of the curve. (Convey confidence, competency, warmth, and sincerity)
- Volunteer; it's a great networking opportunity.
- Have a couple awesome short seminars ready to go on a moment's notice and offer to be a last-minute speaker for various organizations.
- Tell everyone within three feet of you what you do. Become a shameless self-promoter!
- Don't waste a precious moment of your time—ever.
- Stay fit and healthy; get good rest. Break vices if you can.
- Listen to upbeat music instead of constant negative news.
- Have a clear vision and let no one rain on your parade.
- Be flexible and willing to try new things if old ones aren't working.
- Be a nice person. Being rude to a receptionist or a secretary is totally unacceptable!

Remember that Selling is the Name of the Game

This is a sales job. Being a financial advisor, whether in a small planning firm located in some rural slice of paradise or in a Wall Street behemoth is a sales job.

It is no secret that the selling aspect and the rejection that accompanies it is the toughest part of this job, and therefore often avoided at all costs!

Many attempts are made to purify the image of the financial advisor to one of the "upscale executive" or "relationship seeker," and have often led to their failure as they misinterpreted their role and position.

The bottom line is this: sales of product, quality client service, and a stellar reputation floats the boat of this business and everything else is secondary—even deals cut in exquisite boardrooms can be broken down into the sales process.

I wish you happiness, fulfillment and success on *your* path to million dollar production!

About the Author

Patti Branco, president of PB Management Solutions, is a financial services industry expert and professional speaker. She enjoys a successful track record that spans more than twenty years in the financial services arena, first as a successful registered representative, rising through the ranks to management, and later as an independent consultant, building and developing investment programs, leaders, and increased revenue in financial institutions.

Her experience stems from sales and sales management as a First Vice President in the bank and brokerage industry, as State Investment Manager for California, responsible for the initial development of a major bank program in "the Golden State." At one point she was responsible for the future success and compliance oversight of over seventy registered reps, several office staff, and multi-million-dollar budgets.

She left Cal Fed Bank in April 1999 to start her own consulting business and hasn't looked back. Her stellar reputation launched her career as a securities industry consultant and as an 'in demand speaker'. She walks the walk and runs the race, helping companies large and small to develop business, people, and peak performance.

Her client list includes: Phil Broyles Top Producer program, Morgan Stanley, Pentagon Federal Credit Union, Horsesmouth.com, Cal Fed Bank, Allstate Financial Services, CUSO Financial Services, *Los Angeles Times,* Union Savings Bank of Ohio, Primevest Financial Services, Conseco Insurance Company, Los Angeles Bar Association, Nationwide Insurance Company, Countrywide Bank, North Island Federal Credit Union, Financial Resources Credit Union and Union Bank of

California, Princess Cruise Lines, Metropolitan Life Insurance Company, Bank of the West, Investment Company of America and others.

Patti is published and widely quoted. She is a professional member of the National Speakers Association (past Programs Chair for the Los Angeles Chapter). She is past VP of the Board for NSA Los Angeles. Patti is active in her community and energetically volunteers when her heartstrings are tugged!

Patti hails from the Dallas, Texas area.

To contact Patti Branco:
Phone: 903-451-9800
Cell: 214-952-6558
Email:_Patti@PattiBrancoSpeaks.com
Email 2: Patbranco@aol.com
Websites:
www.Pattibranco.com
www.Pattibrancospeaks.com

"Start with a dream. Maybe a dream that is personal and small, but worth doing. Then dream a bigger dream. Keep dreaming until your dreams seem impossible to achieve. Then you'll know you are on the right track. Then you'll know you are ready to conjure up a dream big enough to define your future and perhaps your generation's future."

—Vance Coffman, Business Executive